AF180572

HEALTH CARE IN TRANSITION

PUBLIC REPORTING OF HEALTH CARE PERFORMANCE INFORMATION

BEST PRACTICES

ALEXIS PRATT
EDITOR

nova publishers
New York

Copyright © 2015 by Nova Science Publishers, Inc.

All rights reserved. No part of this book may be reproduced, stored in a retrieval system or transmitted in any form or by any means: electronic, electrostatic, magnetic, tape, mechanical photocopying, recording or otherwise without the written permission of the Publisher.

We have partnered with Copyright Clearance Center to make it easy for you to obtain permissions to reuse content from this publication. Simply navigate to this publication's page on Nova's website and locate the "Get Permission" button below the title description. This button is linked directly to the title's permission page on copyright.com. Alternatively, you can visit copyright.com and search by title, ISBN, or ISSN.

For further questions about using the service on copyright.com, please contact:
Copyright Clearance Center
Phone: +1-(978) 750-8400 Fax: +1-(978) 750-4470 E-mail: info@copyright.com.

NOTICE TO THE READER

The Publisher has taken reasonable care in the preparation of this book, but makes no expressed or implied warranty of any kind and assumes no responsibility for any errors or omissions. No liability is assumed for incidental or consequential damages in connection with or arising out of information contained in this book. The Publisher shall not be liable for any special, consequential, or exemplary damages resulting, in whole or in part, from the readers' use of, or reliance upon, this material. Any parts of this book based on government reports are so indicated and copyright is claimed for those parts to the extent applicable to compilations of such works.

Independent verification should be sought for any data, advice or recommendations contained in this book. In addition, no responsibility is assumed by the publisher for any injury and/or damage to persons or property arising from any methods, products, instructions, ideas or otherwise contained in this publication.

This publication is designed to provide accurate and authoritative information with regard to the subject matter covered herein. It is sold with the clear understanding that the Publisher is not engaged in rendering legal or any other professional services. If legal or any other expert assistance is required, the services of a competent person should be sought. FROM A DECLARATION OF PARTICIPANTS JOINTLY ADOPTED BY A COMMITTEE OF THE AMERICAN BAR ASSOCIATION AND A COMMITTEE OF PUBLISHERS.

Additional color graphics may be available in the e-book version of this book.

Library of Congress Cataloging-in-Publication Data

ISBN: 978-1-63482-346-3

Published by Nova Science Publishers, Inc. † New York

CONTENTS

PREFACE

The purpose of this book is to provide practical approaches to designing public reports that make health care performance information clear, meaningful, and usable by consumers. This book includes three reports which focus on the presentation of comparative health care performance data; the background information contained in public reports that frames the decision question, provides a context for using the information, and details the specifics of the data; and the promotion and dissemination of reports. This book also discusses quality reporting on Medicare's compare sites.

Chapter 1 – The purpose of the Best Practices in Public Reporting series is to provide practical approaches to designing public reports that make health care performance information clear, meaningful, and usable by consumers. This report focuses on the presentation of comparative health care performance data

Chapter 2 – A set of provider performance measures and ratings is not enough to create an effective public report. The purpose of this guide is to identify critical explanatory information needed to accurately communicate quality ratings to consumers and motivate them to use the ratings in making informed health care decisions. The guide includes nine evidence-based recommendations and examples to highlight the recommendations. The intended audiences include Chartered Value Exchanges (CVEs) and other community collaboratives. The guide also may be of interest to States, health plans, and purchasers involved in the design, production, dissemination, and promotion of comparative health care quality and cost information for consumers.

Chapter 3 – The purpose of this guide is to help report sponsors promote and disseminate comparative quality reports to the public. The guide contains 10 evidence-based recommendations. Intended audiences include Chartered

Value Exchanges (CVEs) and other community collaborative. The guide also may be of interest to States, health plans, and purchaser and consumer groups involved in the design, production, promotion, and dissemination of comparative health care quality and cost information for consumers.

Chapter 4 – The Centers for Medicare & Medicaid Services (CMS) has been the driving force behind public reporting on health plan and provider performance in the United States for more than a decade. Based on the premise that making performance information available to the public will lead to a more rational health care marketplace, Medicare's *Compare* web tools were designed initially as sites for consumers to find and compare the performance of health plans, physicians, hospitals, home health agencies, nursing homes, and dialysis facilities. The Patient Protection and Affordable Care Act (ACA) of 2010 now directs CMS to further refine and enhance efforts to educate consumers about quality and empower them to manage their health care.

In: Public Reporting of Health Care ... ISBN: 978-1-63482-346-3
Editor: Alexis Pratt © 2015 Nova Science Publishers, Inc.

Chapter 1

BEST PRACTICES IN PUBLIC REPORTING NO. 1: HOW TO EFFECTIVELY PRESENT HEALTH CARE PERFORMANCE DATA TO CONSUMERS*

Judith Hibbard and Shoshanna Sofaer

PURPOSE

The purpose of the Best Practices in Public Reporting series is to provide practical approaches to designing public reports that make health care performance information clear, meaningful, and usable by consumers. This series consists of three reports:

- Report 1: This report focuses on the presentation of comparative health care performance data.
- Report 2: (Maximizing Consumer Understanding of Public Comparative Quality Reports: Effective Use of Explanatory Information): This report focuses on the background information contained in public reports that frames the decision question, provides

* This is an edited, reformatted and augmented version of AHRQ Publication No. 10-0082-EF, issued by the Agency for Healthcare Research and Quality, June 2010. The document was prepared under contract.

a context for using the information, and details the specifics of the data.

- Report 3 (How To Maximize Public Awareness and Use of Comparative Quality Reports Through Effective Promotion and Dissemination Strategies): This report focuses on the promotion and dissemination of reports.

Together the three reports cover the wide range of issues and challenges faced by report sponsors. The audiences for the three reports are community collaboratives and others involved in the production, packaging, promotion, and dissemination of comparative health care quality and cost information for consumers, patients, and the general public. The goal is to help sponsors present information so that it can be understood easily and processed by people who may have limited time or motivation and are without technical training in this area.

IMPORTANCE OF REPORTING TO THE PUBLIC

Consumers have been slow to use comparative performance reports to make health care choices. Their use of reports, however, can influence quality in at least three ways:

- Informed choices make it more likely that consumers will obtain high-quality health care for themselves and their family members.
- The collective effect of many informed choices may stimulate quality improvement among providers. That is, providers may be motivated to improve as a way to protect or enhance their market share.
- Public reports that affect providers' public image by identifying them as high-quality or low-quality providers may encourage them to improve the quality of care they provide, to protect or enhance their reputations.

Finding ways to make public reports more relevant and useful to consumers is part of an overall strategy to improve health care.

CHALLENGES IN DESIGNING A REPORT CARD

Consumers Do Not Know That There Is a Quality Gap

All of us have heard over and over again that the United States has the best medical care in the world. At the same time, messages about the significant and pervasive quality gaps in health care have been much less omnipresent. It is not surprising that there is a widespread belief among consumers that the technical quality of care is high and uniform across physicians, hospitals, and other providers. If the technical quality of care were actually uniformly high, as many believe, then ignoring public performance reports would make sense. Consumers know, from their own experiences, that the interpersonal aspects of health care do vary considerably. Pairing information on the technical aspects of quality with patient experience data may show consumers that quality is a concept they know something about and can learn more about.

Consumers and Clinical Experts Define Quality Differently

In a national survey, the top three factors that consumers identified as being "most important" in determining the quality of health care patients receive were: affordability of care, doctor's qualifications, and access to care for everyone (Kaiser Family Foundation, 2004). This is quite different from the more multifaceted concept of health care quality represented in most public performance reports that typically include technical quality of care measures as well as patient experience measures. This means there is a serious communication gap between what is contained in reports and what consumers think quality of care means.

Quality Measures Are Often Hard to Understand or Are Not Meaningful to Consumers

Measures of quality are frequently misinterpreted. Misunderstanding takes many forms, and sometimes measures are interpreted in exactly the opposite way they are intended. For example, some hospital reports include length of stay (LOS) or readmissions as performance indicators. Longer LOS and higher readmissions are intended to indicate poor performance. However, many consumers will view these as measures of access and interpret them in the opposite way—they may think that a high score shows that patients are able to stay in the hospital for as long as they need or be readmitted when necessary.

Some measures are incomprehensible to consumers. For example, reporting on measures such as administration of beta blockers and angiotensin-converting enzyme (ACE) inhibitors assumes a higher level of clinical knowledge than most consumers have.

What is not understood is often ignored or viewed as unimportant. The assumption that consumers will "click through" to learn or look up the meaning of an indicator is faulty. If labels are not clear to begin with, they are likely to be ignored.

Using Quality Information to Inform Choices Is Hard Cognitive Work

Using performance reports to inform choices involves reviewing and processing a large amount of information and then applying that information to a choice. As the number of pieces of information or decision factors to consider increases, an individual's ability to use that information to make their choices decreases. Indeed, giving people a lot of information can be counterproductive (Vaiana and McGlynn, 2002; Hibbard, Slovic, and Jewett, 1997). Humans can only integrate a limited number of factors into a choice. When asked, consumers often indicate they want more information. When faced with using that information in making a choice, however, they feel overwhelmed by the amount of information.

Making tradeoffs among different categories of factors (e.g., a doctor who communicates well but whose patients wait long times for appointments) are very difficult cognitive tasks. Most providers are not going to score well on everything, necessitating tradeoffs and differential weighting of factors. Differential weighting of factors in a choice is problematic for people.

Most performance reports are constructed on the assumption that different people will care about different elements of care. The inclusion of multiple performance measures on different elements of care in one report is typically done so that people can pick and choose and differentially weight factors according to their preferences. In reality, people have a very hard time differentially weighting, and even when they think they are doing so, they often are not (Hibbard and Peters, 2003).

In sum, using comparative data to select a provider involves three tasks. Consumers must process a large amount of information, select relevant factors and differentially weight them, and bring all the factors together into a choice. However, research shows that these are very onerous cognitive tasks at which human beings are not very adept.

Thus, for a variety of reasons, consumers have not been quick to use these reports. In addition to all the reasons cited above, reports have not provided guidance on how to act on the information. Finally, consumers are inundated on a daily basis with other kinds of information and demands on their attention. Figuring out what to pay attention to and what is credible information can be additional challenges for them.

PRACTICAL REPORT DESIGN SOLUTIONS

Make the Information More Relevant to What Consumers Already Understand and Care About

1. Present an Overall Definition of Quality

Because consumers do not understand quality of care in the same way that it is often measured and reported, communicating an overall definition that is understandable and salient may help consumers see the relevance of the information. Further, because consumers tend to define quality of care narrowly (e.g., understanding it in terms of the quality of the relationship with their clinician), broadening their concept of quality is likely a necessary prerequisite to making comparative performance information meaningful.

Consumers have a relatively easy time understanding patient experience measures and some patient safety measures. They have a much harder time understanding and relating to process of care measures, volume measures, and many structural measures. Even some classic outcome measures, such as mortality, may be rejected by some consumers, in part because they do not want to think about such a negative idea.

2. Define the Elements of Quality and Use Them As the Reporting Categories

A definition of quality of care that is communicated in everyday language and kept to a few simple ideas will likely work best. For example, phrases using a modified Institute of Medicine framework such as "care that is proven to work," "care that is responsive to a patient's needs," and "care that does not cause harm" communicate what is meant by quality without using jargon or technical terms. Sponsors should consider using these same categories, or ones like them, to frame the decision about choosing a provider, as well as to label overarching reporting categories for displaying the indicators.

The indicators included under the reporting categories also must be salient and easy to understand (and relate to the overarching framework). That is, the indicators too must be in everyday language and speak to the things consumers already care about. For example, "effective and appropriate treatment" is easier to understand than the label "ACE inhibitors." By allowing users to drill down or otherwise find details on the measure, reports can still make specifics available without burdening most users, who will be perfectly happy with the more general label. When reports have categories or category names that are difficult to understand or are viewed as meaningless, sponsors risk discouraging the use of public reports or having users draw inappropriate conclusions about the meaning of the data.

3. Include Information on Sponsor and Methods

The information in reports must be viewed as credible and sponsored by a trusted source. Generally, consumers prefer information from their own physician or from sources that are independent, objective, and knowledgeable. Consumers mistrust information when it appears to come from the organization being evaluated. This means giving full information on sponsorship and methodologies, as well as access to the more granular data. It also requires providing assurances that the information comes from a trusted and reliable source. Such assurances should not be on the "top layer" but need to be available, and made known to be available, in a drill-down layer.

Make It Easy for Consumers to Understand and Use the Comparative Information

1. Reduce the Cognitive Burden by Summarizing, Interpreting, Highlighting Meaning, and Narrowing Options

How much information is presented and the way that information is presented and displayed will make a difference in whether consumers can actually process it and use it in decisionmaking. Among other things, this means being consistent in whatever metrics are used. When a high number (or long bar) indicates good performance with one type of indicator and poor performance with another indicator, the chances of confusing or misleading people is increased. It is always a good idea to make it clear whether a high value means good or bad performance.

Information displays that help consumers quickly see the meaning in the data increase motivation to use the data and actual use of the data. This means summarizing information and even interpreting data for consumers. One of the more powerful display strategies is to rank order providers by performance, with the top performers at the top and the bottom performers at the bottom. Even if the providers are ordered within tiers, where providers within a tier are roughly equal performers, this helps consumers immensely by reducing the work required to make a choice. Ordering by performance also helps to highlight for the user differences in performance.

Labeling performance helps consumers the same way. Labeling performance as "excellent" or "good" does some of the cognitive work for viewers by telling them what the data mean, and even calling out for them outstanding examples. As an example, Figure 1 shows performance with high performers at the top and low performers at the bottom. The summary bar reflects the percentage of indicators for which the physician scored in the 70th percentile or above. If physicians were listed in some other order (e.g., by last name, by ZIP code, by clinic affiliation), consumers would have to review all performance results, doing the difficult cognitive work of identifying and arranging the different performance levels to make a choice.

Figure 2 shows how to present data that include *more than one variable*, such as cost and quality. Here, the "Best Value" label reflects the rater's evaluation of multiple factors and reduces the burden for users, allowing users to identify the top performers regardless of the order in which they are presented.

Using symbols that are inherently meaningful also can help people quickly discern the meaning of data. About one-half of the population has difficulty deriving meaning from numbers. Facing a sea of numbers can be daunting for them, so using symbols rather than numbers can help. The best symbols are those that tell the meaning as part of the symbol.

The examples in Figure 3 show symbols that incorporate the interpretive label as part of the symbol; they incorporate a shape and a color into the symbol so that it is easy to see patterns in the data. When symbols are presented this way, users will be able to immediately interpret them without the added burden of holding information in one's mind as one looks at a legend.

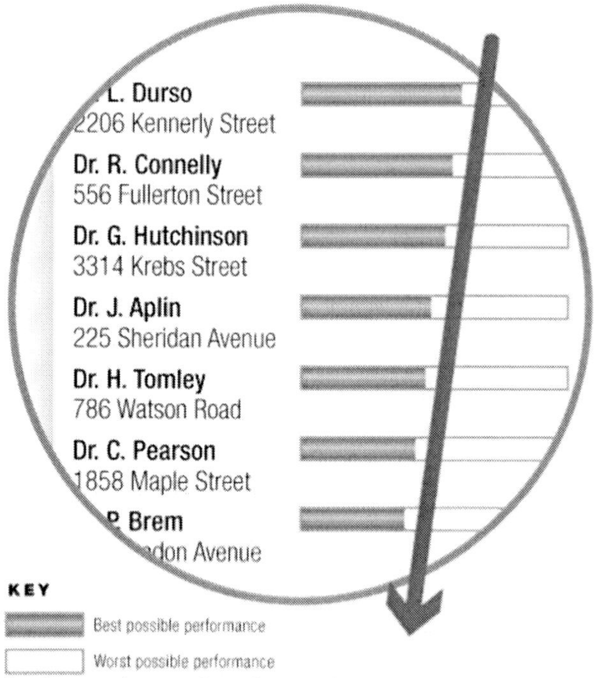

Recommended: Summarize and order performance results to help bring the information together for the user.

* Physician names and addresses are fictitious.

Figure 1. Sample performance report ranking physicians.*

		Consumer Ratings of Health Plan	Provides Excellent Preventive Care	Monthly Premium
	Advantage Plus	★ ★ ★ ★	★ ★ ★	$95
	Health Advantage	★ ★ ★ ★	★ ★ ★ ★	$80
	Health-Net	★ ★ ★ ★	★ ★ ★	$85
	Secure Health	★ ★ ★	★ ★	$100

Recommended: Create a report that summarizes and interprets information for consumers.

* Provider names are fictitious.

Figure 2. Sample report with multiple variables.*

2. Reduce the Cognitive Burden by Helping to Bring the Information Together into a Choice

Many of the strategies discussed above will help users bring the information together into a choice. Any strategies that narrow options, highlight differences, and help the user differentially weight factors will help them arrive at a choice. Using summary measures, and symbols to represent them, helps people “count up” the good attributes. This is the way that most people will use the data, rather than differentially weighting according to personal preferences. Providing them with this framework will help them use the data in decisionmaking.

Making full use of Web-based data allows the user to narrow down the number of data points in a variety of ways. For example, to look only at options in one’s geographic region is the simplest approach. Web-based information may be manipulated a number of ways and customized by users to narrow and order their choices. A PDF file, by contrast, even though simpler to produce, does not allow this customization and is therefore less preferred than a Web-based approach.

Recommended: Use colors, symbols, and simple words to help consumers process and interpret data quickly.

Figure 3. Example of symbols in reports.

Finally, even though it is often technically correct to present confidence intervals when presenting comparative performance data, it should be avoided. To understand the concept of confidence intervals, consumers would need statistical knowledge. Research shows that consumers tend to discount information when a report communicates that there is uncertainty about the data (Schapira, Nattinger, and McHorney, 2001). Confidence intervals should be used to determine performance levels; however, consumers should not be burdened with interpreting them.

Ironically, those characteristics of reports that help consumers the most (e.g., ordering by performance) are also the ones that are most often resisted by providers. Summarizing and interpreting data for consumers, while helping users, puts a greater responsibility on report sponsors. This responsibility may be to determine what constitutes meaningful differences among providers, or to put labels on performance, indicating what levels of performance should be interpreted as good or poor.

Test Reports with Consumers During Development

While we can do our best to produce reports we think consumers will understand and find meaningful, it is always best to test the information with consumers. Such tests will reveal areas consumers do not understand, specific misinterpretations, difficulty users have finding information within reports, and users' perception of the information's relevance. These tests can be done with a small number of consumers, preferably with members of the population who will have access to the report.

Consumer input can be obtained through a variety of questions and tasks. Getting individuals to say in their own words what they think a label or a phrase means reveals quite a lot about their comprehension. Asking people to find the top three and bottom three performing providers will indicate how easy it is for people to put this information together and interpret it correctly. Asking about whether they would use this information to choose a doctor or hospital will reveal how much it is valued.

Research Identifies Critical Design Elements

A recent experiment showed what helped consumers the most:

- Rank ordering by performance as opposed to alphabetical ordering
- Using symbols (such as the ones shown in Figure 3) instead of numbers
- Providing an overall summary measure
- Including fewer reporting categories (5 vs. 9)

The findings showed that with all four of these things, the best results are obtained: 89% of consumers who viewed reports with all four of these design approaches were able to correctly identify the top three and bottom three performers. Only 16% of consumers who viewed the same information with none of these design characteristics could do this.

—Carman KL. Improving quality information in a consumer-driven era: showing differences is crucial to informed consumer choice. 10th National CAHPS User Group Meeting, Baltimore, MD, 2006

COST AND EFFICIENCY

Cost

Increasingly, we are seeing the inclusion of cost data in public reports. While useful to consumers, cost information adds complexity to the choices and can be misleading. Aside from issues of accuracy and reliability of the data, there is a major concern with the interpretation of cost data. Typically, American consumers believe that a more expensive "anything" is of higher quality. If they get cost data alone, without quality data, consumers are likely to use the cost data as a proxy for quality.

Alternatively, reports can show quality within cost strata, or cost within quality strata. In this context, it is easier for the consumer to see that it is possible to get good quality at a good price. An example is a comparison report on care systems from the Patient Choice program offered by Medica Health Plans: http://www.pchealthcare.com/consumers/midwest_ patient choice/ about pcs/ consumersurvey.html. However, if quality information is not well understood or is not integrated with presentation of cost information (e.g., quality within cost strata), misinterpretations may lead to the choice of higher cost options.

Efficiency

Efficiency is not an attribute of health care that consumers are familiar with, nor are they looking for it. The term does not resonate well with consumers, and it can evoke concerns about medical care that is cutting corners or saving money for their health plan or their employer at the consumer's expense. At this point, we do not have a way to effectively communicate with consumers about this issue. Labeling a provider as "efficient" will likely not be viewed as a positive attribute. It will be necessary to test different ways of conveying the concept that will resonate with consumers. For example, "uses health care dollars wisely," "is careful with your health care dollars," or "is a high-value provider" may work better with consumers than the term "efficient." However, whatever is used needs to be tested with consumers first.

Issues Addressed in Reports 2 and 3

Report #2

- How to get started with public reporting.
- How to make the information in reports actionable.
- How to highlight the fact that quality differences exist.
- How to integrate cost and/or efficiency data with quality data.

Report #3

- How to increase the credibility of the reports.
- How to promote the reports.

References and Resources

2006 survey: what consumers want to know about their HMOs. Policy Brief. Sacramento, CA: Center for Health Improvement; September 2006. Available at: http://www.chipolicy.org/doc.asp?id=6059.

TalkingQuality: Guidance for sponsors of consumer reports on health care quality. Rockville, MD: Agency for Healthcare Research and Quality. Available at: http://www.talkingquality.gov/.

Carman KL. Improving quality information in a consumer-driven era: showing the differences is crucial to informed consumer choice. Presentation at the 10th National CAHPS User Group Meeting, Baltimore, MD, 2006.

Hibbard JH, Peters EM. Supporting informed consumer health care decisions: data presentation approaches that facilitate the use of information in choice. *Ann. Rev. Pub. Hlth.* 2003;24:413-33.

Hibbard JH, Slovic P, Jewett JJ. Informing consumer decisions in health care: implications from decision-making research. *The Milbank Quarterly* 1997;75(3):395-414.

National survey on consumers' experiences with patient safety and quality information. Menlo Park, CA: Kaiser Family Foundation; 2004. Available at: http://www.kff.org/kaiserpolls/7209.cfm.

Kanouse D, Spranca M, Vaiana M. Reporting about health care quality: a guide to the galaxy. *Health Promot. Pract.* 2004;5(3):222-31.

Schapira MM, Nattinger AB, and McHorney CA. 2001. Frequency or Probability? A Qualitative Study of Risk Communication Formats Used in Health Care, *Medical Decision Making*, 21: 459-467.

Shaller Consulting. Consumers in health care: creating decision support tools that work. Oakland: California HealthCare Foundation; 2006. Available at: http://www.chcf.org/publications/2006/06/consumers-in-health-care-creating-decisionsupport-tools-that-work.

Shaller Consulting. Designing consumer guides on quality for Medi-Cal managed care beneficiaries. Oakland: California HealthCare Foundation; 2003. Available at: http://www.chcf.org/topics/medical/index.cfm?itemID=20536.

Shaller D. Consumers in health care: the burden of choice. Oakland: California HealthCare Foundation. 2005. Available at: http://www.chcf.org/topics/view.cfm?itemID=115327.

Vaiana ME, McGlynn EA. What cognitive science tells us about the design of reports for consumers. *Med. Care Res. Rev.* 2002;59:3-35.

In: Public Reporting of Health Care ... ISBN: 978-1-63482-346-3
Editor: Alexis Pratt © 2015 Nova Science Publishers, Inc.

Chapter 2

BEST PRACTICES IN PUBLIC REPORTING NO. 2: MAXIMIZING CONSUMER UNDERSTANDING OF PUBLIC COMPARATIVE QUALITY REPORTS: EFFECTIVE USE OF EXPLANATORY INFORMATION*

Shoshanna Sofaer and Judith Hibbard

PURPOSE

A set of provider performance measures and ratings is not enough to create an effective public report. The purpose of this guide is to identify critical explanatory information needed to accurately communicate quality ratings to consumers and motivate them to use the ratings in making informed health care decisions. The guide includes nine evidence-based recommendations and examples to highlight the recommendations. The intended audiences include Chartered Value Exchanges (CVEs) and other community collaboratives. The guide also may be of interest to States, health plans, and purchasers involved in the design, production, dissemination, and

---

* This is an edited, reformatted and augmented version of AHRQ Publication No. 10-0082-1-EF, issued by the Agency for Healthcare Research and Quality, June 2010. The document was prepared under contract.

promotion of comparative health care quality and cost information for consumers.

Value of Effective Public Reports

To date, relatively few consumers have seen comparative performance reports or used them to make health care choices, such as selecting a physician or hospital. [1] Consumer use of reports, however, has the potential to influence quality in at least three ways:

1. Provider performance information makes it more likely that consumers will understand the dimensions of quality and tap this growing understanding in obtaining high-quality health care for themselves and their family members.
2. The collective effect of many informed consumer choices may stimulate quality improvement among providers as they perceive that performance data can affect their market shares.
3. Public reports that affect providers' public image by clearly identifying them as high-quality or low-quality providers may encourage them to improve the quality of care they provide, to protect or enhance their reputations.

Finding ways to make public reports relevant and useful to consumers is part of an overall strategy to improve health care. This report, which is organized around a set of nine recommendations, is intended to help report card sponsors, including CVEs, achieve this goal.

How Explanatory Information Makes a Report More Effective

Most Americans have some experience using data to compare products and services, but public reports of health care quality are not yet in the mainstream. Many people are unaware of their availability, and a large number of those reports have not been easy to understand and use. Evidence and experience make it clear, however, that report designers need to provide explanatory information, in addition to the actual comparative data, to maximize a report's use and impact. This report addresses this need. Whether information is presented online or in print, the right kind of explanatory information will:

1. Engage and motivate consumers to explore and use reports.
2. Deepen consumers' understanding of health care quality and quality measures.
3. Legitimize the report's sponsor and the report's credibility.
4. Provide information about the importance, meaning, and interpretation of specific measures.
5. Help consumers understand the implications of "resource use" information.
6. Help consumers avoid common pitfalls that lead to misinterpreting quality data.
7. Provide consumers guidance and support in using the information.
8. Provide consumers appropriate access to more detailed technical information.

To help achieve these eight aims, report card sponsors are encouraged to:

9. Test the report before going live.

The rest of this report examines these nine recommendations and offers guidance on how to develop and present appropriate explanatory information.

Recommendation No. 1: Engage and Motivate Consumers to Explore and Use Reports

Americans are inundated with information. In the same way that advertisers need to work to get their messages heard above the clutter, [2] sponsors of health care quality reports must give the public compelling reasons to pay attention to their data. Although many consumers have expressed (in focus groups, for example) considerable interest in quality data, that needs to be taken with a grain of salt. When people hear about a new source of information in a focus group, they are likely to find it interesting. But then life happens. People get busy, they are not reminded of the benefits of quality data, and the information loses salience. This does not mean that it is impossible to get people interested in comparative quality information. It does mean that their interest can never be taken for granted, but rather has to be developed and encouraged.

The first page of a report is critical. Once a user arrives at the first page—whether it is printed or online—there are just a few seconds to motivate that person to keep looking rather than moving on to something else or "surfing away," in the case of an online report. A few concisely stated key messages, emphasizing why this information is important and relevant to the consumer, can effectively capture a consumer's attention. Some examples are:

- The quality of the care among (insert facility type and community) can vary widely.
- Consumers who do not look at provider ratings are more likely to make a poor choice.
- A poor choice may have serious consequences for a person's health and finances.
- The information in the report can be useful in selecting a high-quality or high-value provider.
- The information also can be used in other ways (e.g., to help loved ones make a choice, to start a conversation with their doctor or another health professional).

The first page of the "Model Report" shown in Figure 1 is an example from an evidence-based comparative quality report that has been extensively tested and reviewed by experts. It was developed to report on the AHRQ Quality Indicators, a set of measures of hospital quality based on administrative data collected by most States.

Since this is not a "real" report, it does not have a graphic theme or "look." Its intent is to convey the content and language of a report. The key points include:

- A brief definition of quality in consumer-oriented language
- The reasons for publishing comparative data on hospital quality
- Several reasons an individual should look at this information
- A brief summary of the information in the report

Subheads and bullets break up blocks of text. A link at the bottom of the page immediately takes the user to the data. The rest of the report contains a lot more explanatory information, which is either wrapped around the data presentations or positioned at the end of the report.

Recommendation No. 2: Deepen Consumers' Understanding of Health Care Quality and Quality Measures

Consumers and health professionals understand quality issues related to health care differently. Health professionals typically see health care quality as multifaceted; some aspects viewed as critical by professionals are not, initially, seen the same way by consumers. For example, professionals see clinical process measures (e.g., providing a prescription for a beta blocker to patients discharged from the hospital after a heart attack) as critical components of quality and need little in the way of explanatory information. But consumers generally are not familiar with the evidence that links clinical processes to patient outcomes, which consumers care deeply about (e.g., not having another heart attack).

What is to be done about this difference in perspective? First, it is important to recognize that consumers will only find a report useful if it connects to what they already care about. Beyond that, public reports also offer an opportunity to deepen consumers' understanding of health care quality in a way that brings them closer to understanding it as health care professionals do. We need to engage consumers by using explanatory information to make a connection between what they already care about and the more sophisticated elements of quality they could easily come to understand and care about.

Provide a Framework to Help Consumers Understand Quality

One way to increase consumer understanding is to provide a simple, easy-to-understand but comprehensive quality definition or framework that builds on what is known about how consumers and patients define quality. An excellent quality framework that is generally accepted among health professionals already exists in the form of the "six aims" of health care articulated in the Institute of Medicine's report *Crossing the Quality Chasm.* [3] Care should be: (1) safe, (2) effective, (3) timely, (4) patient centered, (5) efficient, and (6) equitable.

A simplified version of this framework was tested with consumers and seems to work well. [4] The concept of safe care is described as "care that protects patients from errors and harm"; the concept of effective care is captured in the phrase "care that is proven to work"; and the phrase "care that is responsive to a patient's needs and preferences" reflects much of what is implied by "patient-centered," "timely," and even "equitable."

Report on Hospital Quality in [community/state]

Quality in health care, including in hospitals, can be described as "doing the right thing, at the right time, in the right way—and having the best possible results."

This report provides information on how well all the hospitals in [community/state] care for patients with a wide range of health problems. It can:

- Help you choose a hospital for yourself
- Provide useful information for your loved ones if they need hospital care
- Encourage hospitals to improve their quality
- Help everyone learn more about hospital quality

Why should you look at this information?

Don't people get good care in any hospital their doctor recommends? Here are the facts:

- All hospitals do not provide the same quality of care. Some hospitals are better than others.
- A particular hospital might do a very good job on some health problems and not such a good job on other health problems.
- Whenever people go to the hospital, they risk getting a new health problem while getting medical care for an existing problem. Hospitals vary in how well they protect patients from these risks.
- Your doctor, or the specialist or surgeon he or she recommends, may be highly skilled, but hospital quality also depends on how well all the hospital staff, such as the nurses, take care of you, and on how well the hospital is organized.

Given these facts, our goal is to give you information you can use to increase your chances of getting the best possible hospital care when you need it.

What information is available in the report?

There are two types of information provided in this report:

- How often patients had medical complications while in the hospital
- How often patients died while in the hospital for certain health conditions and operations

This information is provided about [X] hospitals. By looking at this information, you will be able to assess which hospitals have the fewest number of deaths and complications.

There are many ways to judge hospital quality. We are reporting this information because experience shows it is accurate, easily available for most hospitals from their administrative records, and of interest to members of the public.

Select this link to *start comparing hospitals' results.*

Figure 1. Model Report on AHRQ Quality Indicators.

If reporting a full complement of measures, a report sponsor may opt to organize provider ratings into these three categories:

1. Section on "care that protects patients from medical errors and does not cause harm," which would include measures such as surgical infection rates or injuries from falls.
2. Section on "care that is proven to work," which would include measures such as percentage of diabetes patients who receive all five recommended tests regularly.
3. Section on "care that is responsive to a patient's needs and preferences," which would include measures such as patient experience.

For more information about this framework, refer to Best Practices in Public Reporting No. 1.

Make Sure Reports State Clearly Which Aspects of Quality They Cover

Reports need to make clear the aspects of quality they cover. Using everyday language and listing the main categories of quality data included help to orient the reader. For example, a lead-in to a report could spell out that the report contains measures on patient experiences and effectiveness: "In this report, physicians are compared on 'how responsive they are to patients' needs and preferences' and on 'whether they use practices that are proven to work.'"

The following report example (Figure 2) is from Minnesota Community Measurement, a member of Minnesota's CVE. The report's home page offers succinct explanations of the report's purpose and value, as well as of the measures presented and why they were chosen. This particular online report focuses narrowly on physician quality of care for people with diabetes.

Recommendation No. 3: Legitimize the Report's Sponsor and the Report's Credibility

Focus group research on public reporting consistently finds that the public mistrusts quality information if they think the source of that information has an interest, especially a financial interest, in the ratings. Advertising, including provider and health plan advertising, is so ubiquitous that people are naturally wary that quality reports may simply be marketing ploys. Others may be concerned that the report has been developed by purchasers and heath plans to reduce coverage costs. The public needs to know that the data in reports are objective and that the report is sponsored and supported by trustworthy, expert sources.

The most important contributors to a report's credibility are the credibility of the sponsors and how clearly the sponsorship is presented. If a sponsor is well known and trusted by the consumer audience (not just among health professionals), little needs to be done beyond clearly identifying that sponsor. When sponsors are not well known to consumers, it is important to include a brief description or mission statement up front (in as few words as possible, such as the organization's "tag line") with a link to additional information in the back of the report. (Note in Figure 2 that a link to a description of the sponsor is at the bottom of the home page.) Explaining why the sponsor is issuing the report, and that it has no financial interest in the impact of the report on providers, can help reinforce its credibility to consumers.

If the report is sponsored or published by a CVE, the organization or name may not be familiar to consumers. Even if a CVE is not well known, some of its members likely are well known, and their explicit endorsement of the report can be valuable. Provide clearly labeled links to letters of endorsements from well-known organizations in the State or community, for example, via a special tab on the left-hand side of the home page. Make sure, however, that the full range of partners is shown as endorsing the report. If only one group (e.g., the health plan association, the medical society, a major employer) is shown, people might think it is "their" report and, perhaps, biased in "their" direction.

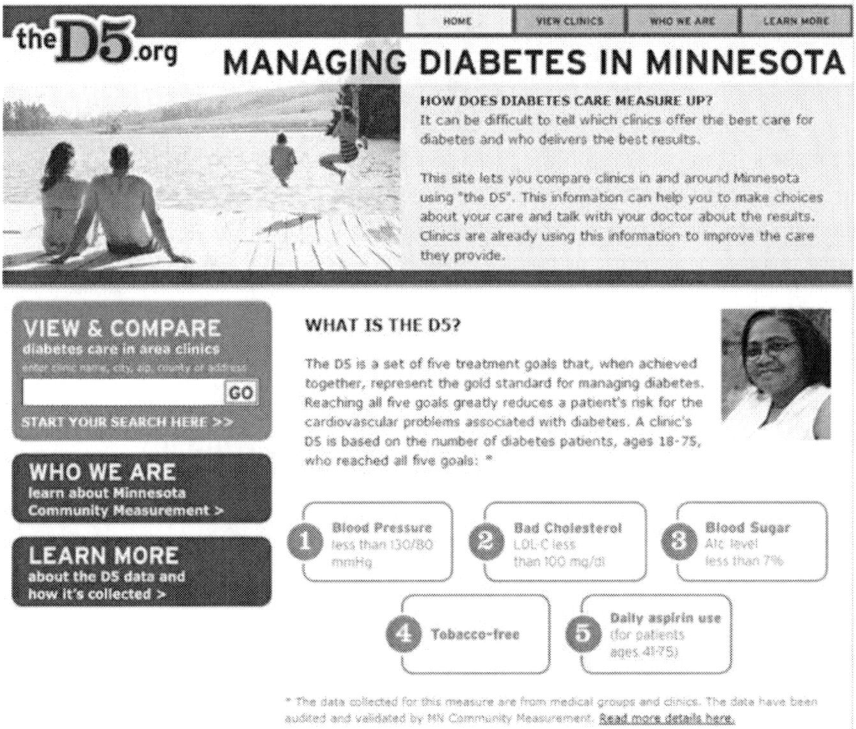

Figure 2. The D5 Web Site Offers a Clear Explanation of Its Purpose and Value.

Establish Credibility by Demonstrating Fairness

The public wants to know that reports are fair to those being rated. Focus group researchers have heard repeatedly that a specific measure is not really the sole responsibility of the entity or individual being assessed. Some consumers say that the responsibility is broader—the patient's, or another health professional's, or shared by multiple professionals.

For example, when older women were asked about the inclusion of a mammography rate in an early HEDIS (Healthcare Effectiveness Data and

Information Set) measurement set used to compare health plans, they thought that either the woman herself or her doctor was responsible for whether she had a mammogram, not the health plan. [5] In response to this feedback, explanatory information was added to the presentation of these data in an early version of Medicare Compare. This information acknowledged that patients and physicians affect a health plan's mammography rate but also specified exactly *how* health plans can act to ensure that more women get needed mammograms.

Another way to demonstrate fairness is by describing key aspects of the sponsor's interactions with the providers who are rated. While it is a good idea to make clear that you are at arm's length with providers, it also can help to: (1) conduct a dry run of data collection and aggregation, which is reported only to providers, prior to the actual public report; and (2) give providers an opportunity to comment on the findings. If you take these steps, tell the public about them, briefly and in plain language.

Provide the Right Level of Detail to Ensure Credibility

Many report designers believe that for the public to trust a report, they need to know a lot of the technical details about how the data were collected and how the scores were generated. In particular, report designers think people need to know the extent to which differences between those rated are statistically or substantially significant. Because of this concern, some designers address statistical significance by including details (e.g., confidence intervals in graphs or highly technical presentations of data) in the main body of the report.

Such complex data presentations are unlikely to be either read or understood. In fact, consumers may see information about adjustments to the data as a sign that someone is "messing with the information." Therefore, it is important to find the right balance between technical details and summary information.

This challenge can be addressed by providing technical details in a special section toward the back of the report (after the measures or ratings). Links to this information should be provided early, however, to signal that the details are available to anyone who wants them. It is appropriate to have links like this throughout the report (e.g., via a tab at the left or on the top of the screen, for an online report) to reinforce the continuous availability of this information, as it is hard to predict when a given individual may want to look at it. Realistically, health professionals are more likely to look at this information than consumers are, but it must be made available to all. Most important, it must be written as clearly and simply as possible; unfamiliar terms need to be defined as they are used.

Technical details provided with the data display should include information about the time period covered by the data and data sources, including mention of whether data provided by the providers or health plans being rated are validated or audited in some way. When survey information is reported, people want to know that the sample was random and reasonably large. They also want to know that the surveys were conducted and scores generated by an independent entity.

Explain How Scores Were Generated

Scoring can make a big difference in the effect comparative data have on consumers' understanding of quality information. For example, when Hospital CAHPS® data are presented on the Hospital Compare Web site, graphs show the percentage of patients in each hospital who gave the best possible rating for a given experience. However, when a composite of several measures is reported (such as, for example, communication between patients and their nurses) the graphs show the percentage of patients in each hospital who gave the best possible report on *ALL* items in the composite.

From a consumer-engagement perspective, it is a good thing if the information shows variation, because it reinforces the idea that there is real variation in quality. On a more fundamental level, it makes people more interested in the information and more likely to think it can help them make a good choice. However, these scoring decisions need to be made clear, both in the individual data presentations and in the technical details.

Another aspect of scoring is risk adjustment or, in some cases, "smoothing" of data through hierarchical modeling when some of the entities being rated are substantially smaller than others. [6,7] These strategies involve complex statistical techniques, and they cannot be presented in public reports using language one might use in a graduate (or even undergraduate) course. The language must be as simple as possible but not so simplistic that the steps taken to ensure accuracy and fairness of the data are unclear.

The authors have found through research that people tend to understand adjustments based on age or severity of illness but react negatively to adjustments based on social factors such as education level. To the extent that a report sponsor plans to stratify data by race, ethnicity, or income level, the authors caution that this will have to be done carefully so that consumers do not see it as a manipulation of the "real" data or discrimination against racial, ethnic, or income groups.

Recommendation No. 4: Provide Information About the Importance, Meaning, and Interpretation of Specific Measures

In addition to providing a broad framework that defines different aspects of quality, reports need to offer simply stated explanations around their graphic presentations of data. They need to describe how the measures relate to quality and, sometimes, how to interpret the graphic.

Use Terms Consumers Understand

Many reports justify using technical terms by including a glossary. People rarely use glossaries, however, and are not likely to examine information they do not understand. If technical terms are used, they must be defined immediately in everyday language that will be understood by individuals at an eighth-grade reading level or lower. An even better strategy is to use a common term (e.g., breast cancer screening test), with the technical term (e.g., mammography) in parentheses.

Ideally, the measures reported will have been vetted previously with consumers to see if they find them important, relevant, and appropriate to the providers or health plans being rated. If a measure has not been formally vetted, it may be necessary to conduct focus groups to obtain input on how to present it. Focus groups were conducted before finalizing the Hospital CAHPS survey, for example. They helped determine which items stayed in the survey and helped inform decisions about the contextual information needed. [8] For more information about testing, refer to "Recommendation No. 9: Test the report with consumers before going live" later in this report.

Explain Different Types of Measures

The explanatory information needed depends on the type of measure, because consumers' interest in and level of understanding of the different types of measures will vary. When developing such information for public reports, consider the following key points about each type of measure:

- *Patient experience measures, such as those derived from CAHPS surveys:* People seem to naturally understand this kind of measure. Most, but not all, people value and will use rating information from other patients and consumers.
- *Outcome measures:* These measures are just beginning to be included in reports. Early testing on these measures with consumers indicates a range of responses to them:
    - *Patient safety measures, such as measures of the frequency of infections, falls, and other negative consequences of care delivery*: Once explained in plain language, these measures seem to resonate with many consumers. It appears important when presenting safety measures to emphasize that specific bad outcomes can be prevented by providers.
    - *Mortality measures:* These elicit a wide range of responses from consumers. Some say they do not want to read or think about the potential of death when they seek medical care. Others believe it is important to have this information, however, particularly for serious illnesses or high-risk procedures. Still others think that simply not dying does not equate to high-quality care. Their definition of quality goes far beyond that to issues of being cured, improving quality of life, or having a positive experience as a patient. Finally, people's interest in a disease- or procedure-specific mortality measure will depend on whether they care about that disease or procedure. It makes sense to include outcome measures in public reports; however, some may require explanatory information, and all must be described in lay terms.
- Clinical process measures: It is almost always necessary to explain these kinds of measures. Clinical processes are not familiar to many consumers, and they rarely know the evidence of how a particular process supports a desirable outcome. The report must use plain language to describe the process, so that the importance is clear (e.g., patient given right medication at right time). The label should help people make the connection between the process and the outcome.

  For example, the HEDIS assessments of health plans include a mammography measure as a key effectiveness indicator. When this measure was introduced, mammography rates were considerably lower than they are now. At that time, many women did not know the benefit of getting a mammogram. They typically thought of it as a test they had to take (and pass) to make sure they did not have breast cancer. However, a much more important benefit of getting a mammogram is that the earlier breast cancer is detected, the greater likelihood that it can be treated successfully, often using less invasive treatments. Explaining this in plain language links mammography rates to outcomes that are important to all women: being cured and having less physical disfigurement.

When these data were first presented, the Centers for Medicare & Medicaid Services (CMS) included an explanation of these benefits in a section of the report called "Why Is This Important?" Further, because women often did not think health plans could do much about a mammography rate, CMS included another section titled "What Does This Measure Show?" that discussed how health plans influence mammography rates.

Provide Guidance on How to Read Graphs and Understand Measures

Often people need to be told what to look for in a graph. For example, they need guidance to understand if a high score or a low score indicates higher performance. A bar on a graph to indicate the average or some other benchmark requires an explanation, as shown in Figure 3.

Recommendation No. 5: Help Consumers Understand the Implications of Resource Use Information

"Resource use" is a broad term, which is intended to include measures of price and efficiency and capture potential inefficiencies such as hospital readmissions. Report sponsors are just beginning to include resource use information in public reports; there are few well-developed measures in this arena. Resource use measures need to be relevant to consumers, but as one might expect, there is not much research yet on what is relevant to them and how the measures should be presented so that they will not be misunderstood. The term "resource use" has not been tested with consumers and is likely to be poorly understood.

Two common consumer beliefs are likely barriers to using cost and efficiency measures effectively. One is the widespread belief that "more care is better." Consumers are much more concerned about not getting something they need than they are about getting care they do not need.

This graph shows you the percentage of patients admitted to each hospital after having a heart attack (called an *acute myocardial infarction*) who died during their hospital stay. This information is for patients admitted during [insert year].

When you are choosing a hospital, you should look for the hospital that has a lower number of deaths. A **lower** number is shown by a **shorter** bar on the graph below.

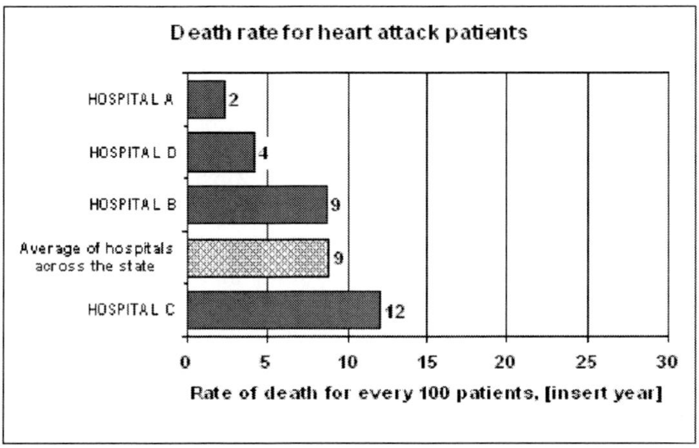

Average of hospitals across the State: The average rate of patients who died after having a heart attack, in hospitals across your State. This number is included so you have:

- A better idea of what is typical for your State.
- A basis for comparing individual hospitals' performance.

Figure 3. A Plain Language Explanation Helps Consumers Interpret Data Quickly.

The second common belief is that price, as with most consumer goods, is a reasonable proxy for quality. That is, when consumers are not getting a clear message about quality, they are likely to use cost as a proxy for quality. This can result in counterproductive choices.

Beginning to address these misconceptions in public reports is a first step in communicating about resource use issues. Keeping these misconceptions in mind as sponsors create approaches for reporting on resource use measures will be essential.

Recommendation No. 6: Help Consumers Avoid Common Pitfalls That Lead to Misinterpretation of Quality Data

While the authors do not recommend providing extensive statistical detail within data presentations, it is important to include caveats about certain measures that could otherwise be misleading. As shown in the examples below, reports must communicate to users:

- That they should use caution in comparing providers on certain measures; and
- That they cannot assess a provider's overall performance by extrapolating from a limited set of measures that reflect only some of the services they provide.

Some patient safety measures address extremely rare events, including "never events." The problem with measures of rare events is that it is difficult to make valid comparisons among providers or health plans. For example, Hospital A reports two deaths in a given year among hip replacement patients, while Hospital B (with about the same number of surgeries and mix of patients) reports one death. Consumers might falsely conclude that Hospital B's performance is twice as good as Hospital A. Since deaths among hip-replacement patients are extremely rare, the difference in rates in a given year may be random—more noise than signal.

Here are some options for addressing this kind of measure:

- Exclude such measures from your report.
- Combine data for multiple years so that the noise diminishes. This means changing the measure from deaths in a single year to deaths over the last 3 years or last 5 years. Even then the rates may be extremely low.
- Aggregate data from one of these measures, such as deaths among hip-replacement patients, with deaths from other low-risk surgeries or procedures.
- Present data on the measure, but add a statement with the data, pointing out that the event is rare and that users should be cautious in comparing facilities or providers on the basis of this measure alone.

If you do report such measures, consider using counts rather than rates. Because so many Americans have limited numeracy, it is difficult for them to grapple with a rate such as 1 death per 10,000 patients or .0001 percent.

Another common misunderstanding is that the measures included in an online or printed report tell the whole story of a given provider's or plan's performance. Consumers may sometimes think they have the whole story and can judge a hospital, for example, based solely on how it performs on measures related to cardiovascular care, even when they are going to the hospital for cancer surgery. This kind of caveat is better presented in a section on how to use the report than near any single data presentation, since it really speaks to the report as a whole.

Recommendation No. 7: Provide Consumers Guidance and Support in Using the Information

We have reviewed how the home page of the report presented on a Web site or the first page of a printed report is a good place to quickly indicate the benefits of a report (i.e., how it can be used by consumers). Additional "decision support information" can be helpful in providing guidance and motivation for those who are not familiar with or are less confident in using quality information for themselves or their loved ones.

In many cases, the desired primary use of comparative quality information is to influence consumer choice. Simply providing information, however, is not sufficient. Many believe that "decision support" must be included in reports. [9] For example, reports often provide information on a wide range of measures but do not address how to put all the information together to make a decision. The cognitive burden of this task is extremely high for almost anyone. [10]

Efforts have been made to provide formal decision support within online reports by asking individual users what is most important to them and then using internal functionality to calculate the available options that best meet their preferences. This is a complex undertaking, made more difficult by the fact that many health care consumers find it hard to identify the aspects of quality that are most important to them.

Following are five simple, practical approaches to providing decision support for consumers:

1. Provide a list of what consumers should think about when they make a decision of this kind. This list can include issues related to information covered in the report, but it may include issues other than quality, such as convenient location or languages spoken by staff. For example, the report could list several things to consider in choosing a primary care physician, such as how well each communicates with patients, how easy it is to make an appointment and whether the physician provides needed preventive services on time, and whether the physician delivers the right care to patients with specific conditions.

   Going beyond typical quality measures, the list might also include whether the physician's office is located conveniently for the person, whether the physician is included in the network of the patient's health plan or accepts the patient's insurance, and whether the physician speaks a language other than English. If consumers are urged or required to gather information from outside sources, the report should contain links or other directions on how to access that information. This kind of simple decision support has been shown to be highly valued by many consumers. [11]
2. Identify, through a label or a visual such as a checkmark, which of the choices is the "best scoring" across the board or the "best value" if cost data also are included. Consumer Reports has used this approach for many years. This kind of label operates like a summary score.

   Composite scores, common in survey-based measures, can be helpful in reducing the total number of data points in a report, but they do not help as much as summary or "roll-up" scores. Unlike composite scores, summary or "roll-up" scores combine a large number of specific measures that may or may not be highly related to one another statistically. They relate to a single provider or facility. Consumers often say they want summary or "roll-up" scores, which can make it easier for consumers to evaluate choices and make decisions.

   Two issues must be addressed in developing and reporting summary or "roll-up" scores, however. First, it is important not to wash out any variation across providers—something that will make it harder for consumers to make a decision. Summary scores that reveal that some providers and facilities are better across the board can be extremely helpful to consumers.

Second, care must be taken in weighting items in summary scores (i.e., giving more weight to some measures than to others). For example, it might seem obvious on the face of it to assign greater weight to a measure of the number of patients who die from central-line infections versus another measure of how quiet a hospital is at night. It is not clear, however, what the right weighting would be for any number of measures, and it is inevitable that different consumers will weight a set of measures differently.

3. Call out key differences in performance, (i.e., pointing out places where differences in scores are particularly large).
4. Provide examples of specific ways consumers can use information, not just for making personal health care choices, but also to learn more about what kind of care is high quality, to help loved ones make a decision, or to begin a conversation with their physician or other provider. Stories and testimonials can illustrate how information can be applied (e.g., including first-person statements by consumers about how using the report made a difference in their choices, health, or finances).
5. Make explicit what actions consumers can take to protect themselves from poor-quality care. The most obvious step consumers can take is to avoid choosing and using poor-quality providers. Sometimes, as we know, consumers have little or no choice of health plans or hospital. One step a consumer might take in this case would be to talk about the issue of poor hospital quality with his or her physician.

   In recent research, physicians were asked how they would respond if patients expressed concerns about hospital quality information they had seen in a public report. [12] While many physicians said they would try to reassure their patient about the quality of the hospital, many also said they would alert the involved specialist about the patient's concerns, be vigilant about specific concerns while on rounds, or speak to the nursing staff or, in some cases, hospital executives. A few physicians said they would encourage the patient and family to be proactive in monitoring the patient's care and to make it clear when they thought something was not going as it should. This research implies that consumers can and should talk to their doctors about quality concerns.

Recommendation No. 8: Provide Consumers Appropriate Access to More Detailed Technical Information

People can become overwhelmed and give up on a report if they cannot find what they are looking for. Report design should use layering and navigation aids so that users are not overwhelmed with information or required to look at information that is of lesser interest to them. In general, this means report designers need to balance the consumer's need for brevity and ease of access to what they care about most with the sponsor's need to provide full descriptions, caveats, and disclosures about the data. Using the Web to disseminate reports makes creating this balance much easier than in print reports.

A good Web site report incorporates several features to help people know where they are and get where they want to go:

- A set of tabs at the top to help users get to the main sections from anywhere in the report
- A set of tabs at the side to help users navigate within report sections
- Internal links from one part of the report to another

The amount of explanatory information provided up front should be limited, unless there is a special reason for breaking this rule. (For an example of such a case, see Figure 4.)

We recently created and tested a *Model Report on Hospice Quality*. Our initial focus group research confirmed that the public does not understand what a hospice is or what it does. Indeed, they have serious misconceptions that might make it impossible for them to understand available quality measures about hospice. For example, to many people hospice is a place, a facility where people go. In fact, the vast majority of people use hospice services in their own homes, where they are visited by a wide range of hospice team members.

In response to this feedback, our *Model Report* included extensive information about the nature of hospice, both up front and at the back. Even so, we gave users the option on the report home page to explore this information if they chose or to go right to the data. Keep in mind that users may start with the data and then return to the more educational components of the site, especially if they have the right navigational cues wherever they are.

Figure 4. Example of a Case When More Up-Front Information Is Useful [13].

Explanatory information that is best located toward the back of a report includes:

1. Technical details of how data are collected and analyzed
2. Methods to provide feedback or ask questions about the report
3. Letters of endorsement
4. More detailed information about how to use the report such as described in Recommendation No. 7
5. Things to keep in mind while using the data (this is where the caveats go)
6. Links to other reports on quality that cover aspects not covered in the current report
7. Additional resources and links on topics relevant to the report (e.g., information about diseases or conditions if the report is organized that way)
8. Contact information for rated providers and health plans, if the number is small

Although every report does not need to include all of the above, the first and second items are the most important to include. Even if consumers do not look at the technical details, they like to know they are there. Their advocates, as well as other stakeholders, will look at these details carefully.

Last, but definitely not least, offering a vehicle for feedback reinforces the idea that the sponsor is open to improvement and provides a quick and inexpensive way to get information to evaluate the effectiveness of the report. Allowing users to ask questions may be helpful in situations where consumers need clarification about different reports on the same provider or plan.

Recommendation No. 9: Test the Report with Consumers before Going Live

Report format, language, and structure should be tested with consumers. This sounds daunting, but it does not have to be. The best way to test is through cognitive interviews. [14] This technique was initially created to assess survey questionnaires to make sure potential respondents would consistently understand questions and possible response options as the survey developers intended. Cognitive interviews are the gold standard in survey testing. For more than a dozen years, cognitive interviews have been used to test public reports to ensure that consumers understand them as intended, that they can navigate their way around them, and that they are likely to respond positively to the content and how it is presented.

Conduct Cognitive Tests

Use a draft that looks as much as possible like the potential Web site or printed report. Then develop a protocol for cognitive testing and recruit 10 to 15 subjects who reflect a cross-section of the intended audience. Each test should take about 90 minutes and involve three persons—a subject, an interviewer, and a note taker—where possible. Tape-recording each interview is recommended. Watch for parts of a page where the respondent spends more time or less time, when they seem confused, etc. It is helpful to offer a financial incentive to subjects for their participation, ranging from $75 to $125, depending on the local cost of living. Saturation (where little more can be learned) is reached after 10 to 15 individual cognitive tests.

The key to a good cognitive test is to guide people, step by step, through the report, get their reactions to it, and ask questions to find out if they understand both the text and the graphics. Do not ask people if they understand; rather, ask them a knowledge question and see if they respond with the correct information. For example, ask them to identify the highest and lowest performers, to characterize the main point of a section of text, to discuss why an average is included, or to describe where the data come from. Ask if anything in the report makes them trust or distrust it, where too much or too little has been said.

Do not be surprised if people are brutally honest and if the process turns out to be somewhat painful, especially for those who have agonized over just the right wording and graphics. Refine reports in response to the results of these tests. Schedule two or three rounds of tests, revising the draft report between rounds, if time and money allow.

Disciplined testing and use of evidence-based practices will help improve the likelihood that the report will be understood, appreciated, and most importantly, used.

PURPOSE OF REPORT SERIES

The purpose of this three-part series of reports is to provide practical approaches to designing public reports that make health care performance information clear, meaningful, and usable by consumers. The goal is to help sponsors present information so that a wide variety of people can understand and apply it easily to key decisions, even if they do not want to spend a lot of time on details and have limited technical knowledge of the subject.

Together the three reports cover the wide range of issues and challenges faced by report sponsors:

- *Best Practices in Public Reporting No. 1: How To Effectively Present Health Care Performance Data to Consumers* focuses on the challenges involved in designing a public report card so that the performance information is easily understood by consumers and on strategies to make it easier for consumers to understand and use comparative health care quality reports.
- *Best Practices in Public Reporting No. 2: Maximizing Consumer Understanding of Public Comparative Quality Reports: Effective Use of Explanatory Information* focuses on the explanatory information in public reports, beyond the performance data itself, that helps to accurately communicate quality ratings to consumers and motivate them to use the ratings in making informed health care decisions.

Best Practices in Public Reporting No. 3: How To Maximize Public Awareness and Use of Comparative Quality Reports Through Effective Promotion and Dissemination Strategies applies social marketing and other principles to explore how to target reports to specific audiences, develop messages to promote the report with key audiences, engage consumer advocacy and community groups in promoting reports and helping people use them, disseminate reports through trusted channels, and ensure that consumers see and use comparative quality reports.

REFERENCES

[1] 2008 update on consumers' views of patient safety and quality information. Menlo Park, CA: *Kaiser Family Foundation*; October 2008.

[2] Shaller Consulting. Consumers in health care: creating decision-support tools that work. Oakland: *California HealthCare Foundation*; June 2006.

[3] Institute of Medicine Committee on Quality Health Care in America. Crossing the quality chasm: a new health system for the 21st century. Washington, DC: *National Academy Press*; 2001. p. 5-6.

[4] Hibbard JH, Pawlson LG. Why not give consumers a framework for understanding quality? *Jt. Comm. J. Qual. Saf.* 2004 June;30(6):347-51.

[5] McGee J, Sofaer S, Kreling B. Findings from focus groups conducted for the National Committee for Quality Assurance (NCQA) Medicare and Medicaid Consumer Information Projects. Washington, DC: *National Committee for Quality Assurance*; July 1996.

[6] Iezzoni LI. Risk adjusting rehabilitation outcomes: an overview of methodological issues. *Am. J. Phys. Med. Rehabil.* 2004 Apr;83(4):316-26.

[7] Shahian DM, Normand ST. Comparison of "risk-adjusted" hospital outcomes. *Circulation* 2008 Apr;117:1955-63.

[8] Sofaer S, Firminger K. Patient perceptions of the quality of health services. *Annu. Rev. Public Health* 2005 Apr;26:513-59.

[9] Spranca M. RAND report summary: consumer use of information when making treatment decisions. Chicago: BlueCross BlueShield Association; 2005.

[10] Peters EM, Hibbard H, Slovic P, et al. Numeracy skill and the communication, comprehension, and use of risk and benefit information. *Health Aff.* 2007;26(3):741-8.

[11] McCormack LA, Garfinkel SA, Hibbard JH, et al. Health insurance knowledge among Medicare beneficiaries. *Health Serv. Res.* 2002;37(1):43-63.

[12] Barr JK, Bernard SL, Sofaer S, et al. Physicians' views on public reporting of hospital quality data. *Med. Care Res. Rev.* 2008 Dec;65(6):655-73; E pub 2008 July 2.

[13] Sofaer S, Hopper SS, Firminger K, et al. Addressing the need for public reporting of comparative hospice quality: a focus group study. *Jt. Comm. J. Qual. Saf.* 2009;35(8):422-9.

[14] Harris-KojetinLD, Fowler FJ, Brown JA, et al. The use of cognitive testing to develop and evaluate CAHPS 1.0 core survey items. Consumer Assessment of Health Plans Study. *Med. Care* 1999;37:MS10-21.

In: Public Reporting of Health Care ...
Editor: Alexis Pratt

ISBN: 978-1-63482-346-3
© 2015 Nova Science Publishers, Inc.

Chapter 3

BEST PRACTICES IN PUBLIC REPORTING NO. 3: HOW TO MAXIMIZE PUBLIC AWARENESS AND USE OF COMPARATIVE QUALITY REPORTS THROUGH EFFECTIVE PROMOTION AND DISSEMINATION STRATEGIES*

Shoshanna Sofaer and Judith Hibbard

PURPOSE

The purpose of this guide is to help report sponsors promote and disseminate comparative quality reports to the public. The guide contains 10 evidence-based recommendations. Intended audiences include Chartered Value Exchanges (CVEs) and other community collaborative. The guide also may be of interest to States, health plans, and purchaser and consumer groups involved in the design, production, promotion, and dissemination of comparative health care quality and cost information for consumers.

---

* This is an edited, reformatted and augmented version of AHRQ Publication No. 10-0082-2-EF, issued by the Agency for Healthcare Research and Quality, June 2010. The document was prepared under contract.

Value of Effective Public Reports

According to a recent poll from the Kaiser Family Foundation, 30 percent of Americans say they have seen information comparing the quality of different insurance plans, hospitals, or doctors, while only 14 percent have used such information. [1] These figures are slightly higher than in surveys conducted in previous years. For example, a 2007 survey by Harris Interactive on behalf of the California HealthCare Foundation revealed that 23 percent of respondents had seen hospital comparative quality reports. [2]

Consumer use of reports can influence quality in at least four ways:

1. Increase consumer understanding of dimensions of quality that are relevant to their needs. Consumers can use their expanding understanding to obtain high-quality health care for themselves and their family members, not only when they choose providers but also when they use health care.
2. Stimulate quality improvement among providers (in more competitive markets) if they perceive that performance data may affect consumer choice and, thus, their market shares.
3. Encourage purchasers and health plans to use higher quality providers in their networks.
4. Affect the public image of clinicians and facilities, by clearly identifying their performance compared to their peers. This has been demonstrated to encourage them to improve the quality of care they provide, to protect or enhance their reputations. [3,4]

As a result, gaining broad awareness of public reports on quality through effective promotion and dissemination is part of an overall strategy to improve health care. This report, which is organized around 10 recommendations, is intended to help report sponsors, including CVEs, achieve this goal.

Why Promotion and Dissemination Are Critical to Effective Public Reporting

It is essential that sponsors enhance public awareness of comparative quality reports and the benefits consumers can derive from using them. Report sponsors invest substantial time and valuable resources in designing and producing comparative quality reports. In the first two reports in this *Best Practices* series, we shared insights into how to produce a report that people can understand and use. But if consumers do not know about public reports, they will never see them. If they never see them, they cannot use them. And if they do not use them, there is no return on those investments.

Few, if any, sponsors have been fully successful in expanding access to and awareness and use of quality reports whether they use a print or Web format. There are several reasons for this problem: poor promotion and dissemination of reports; flagging awareness among consumers who heard an initial announcement about a report and then forgot about it; lack of consumer interest in the providers measured or the measures reported; and poor report design.

Little research exists on how to promote and disseminate quality reports; however, there is much to learn from social marketing and Web marketing. In this report, we will apply key insights and strategies from those fields to the challenges of getting comparative quality reports seen and used by the public. This is a tough job, but there are steps sponsors can take to reach more of the people who need to see and use reports.

In the following sections, we offer 10 recommendations for handling specific challenges:

1. Plan from the outset for promotion and dissemination.
2. Identify your audience as early as possible.
3. Engage those who can help you learn about and reach your audience.
4. Use the insights of social marketing.
5. Be strategic about timing.
6. Be strategic about positioning.
7. Actively work with media to promote the report.
8. Use advertising to promote the report.
9. Use outreach to promote the report and facilitate its use.
10. Gather and analyze feedback on the report and its promotion.

We also encourage report sponsors to share what they learn with each other as they take on this task.

Recommendation No. 1: Plan from the Outset for Promotion and Dissemination

It is critical to address how to promote and disseminate your comparative quality report in the beginning stages of the planning process. Time and resources must be budgeted at the outset as part of the entire public reporting process. In addition, it is best to pursue partnerships that will be important for the end tasks of promotion and dissemination before making major decisions.

Some of the most important resources to help with promotion are people. It will be critical to create a team with expertise in media relations and marketing, especially social marketing; advertising and promotion; and Web-based promotion and analytics. Some CVEs, such as the Puget Sound Health Alliance, have found it useful to create a multistakeholder communication committee that includes representatives from consumer groups, physicians, hospitals, employers, unions, and government agencies.

Many potential partners may have deep experience in these areas that can be applied to promoting comparative quality reports to consumers. For example, private sector purchasers have staff or other resources with marketing, advertising, and Web expertise. The Cincinnati CVE, Health Improvement Collaborative of Greater Cincinnati and HealthBridge, is fortunate to include Proctor & Gamble, a major consumer products firm with extraordinary expertise in marketing. Proctor & Gamble assigned one member of its staff to work with the CVE for 18 months on promotion and dissemination issues. In addition, the company helped the CVE develop its Web site. Public and nonprofit organizations also have expertise in media relations and social marketing, as well as skill at marketing with limited budgets.

In putting together a multistakeholder partnership, it is also imperative to include those who serve, can reach, and are trusted by your audience, in particular consumer and patient organizations. Involve them early and ensure that they have a clear voice in decisions. These organizations are not likely to participate as productively and completely as you would like unless they believe they are viewed as essential to the process, rather than an afterthought.

Recommendation No. 2: Identify Your Audience As Early As Possible

Sponsors must identify, and get to know, their audiences as soon as possible to ensure effective promotion and dissemination of comparative quality reports or cost information.

Whom do you want to reach? Often, sponsors say they want to reach everyone in the community. While this is admirable, it may be self-defeating, at least in the short term. Marketing professionals know that "audience segmentation" is essential for effective promotion of any product or service.

We are a highly diverse society. People's needs and interests differ. A message that reaches older rural Americans, for example, will not necessarily work with the urbanized Facebook generation. Women respond differently than men. People from different ethnic groups have different beliefs and values about health care that will significantly influence both what to emphasize and where to place your messages. The nature of the information provided also points to the audience. Information about primary care physicians implies a broad audience. Data that relates to nursing home quality suggests a narrower audience: those likely to be admitted to a nursing home, plus those who help them make decisions. So, while planning, sponsors should think carefully about priorities in terms of audience. A CVE's mandate is important, but within the context of a mandate for a public report, there are options. Report sponsors may choose to target audiences who:

1. Need the information the most.
2. Will be easiest to motivate to look at and use the information.

These groups are unlikely to overlap completely, so tradeoffs will be necessary.

Reach Those Who Need Your Information the Most

Our first instinct in health care is to help those whose need is greatest. Sponsors may want to target reports to people whose health problems are most pressing and serious. Comparative quality information is likely to be of high interest and significant value for them. They use a disproportionate amount of health care services, so influencing them also has a high potential impact.

People with chronic conditions may be a very important audience, but reaching them is not without challenges. People who are extremely ill may not have the energy and focus to examine comparative quality reports, even those that contain data specific to their condition. This suggests the need for a broad reach to include the people in your audience who help those who are very ill, frail, cognitively impaired, or otherwise unable to use your report.

An ideal audience for public reports on comparative quality is one that contains people who are not seriously ill but who know they will be using health care in the next few months or year. Here are three examples: (1) women who are pregnant or planning to become pregnant very soon; (2) people who are planning to have elective surgery, such as joint replacement, as soon as they absolutely have to but not right away; and (3) people who recently moved to a community and need to find a primary care provider. Even in these cases, you may need to extend the audience to include family members and close friends who can help fragile consumers deal with their health problems.

Target Those Who Are Easy to Reach and Motivate

Evidence indicates that people can be divided into two basic groups, sometimes called "monitors" and "blunters," with respect to their use and processing of information about health. [5,6] Monitors generally want all the information they can get; blunters, if they want to know anything, only want the basics, and may actively want to avoid things that are frightening. Especially at the outset of your reporting efforts, focus on the monitors, while also including information on the "basics" for the blunters. Even information-hungry monitors will look only at information that is *of immediate relevance* to their concerns. They will search for your reports, but they must be easy to find. (Recommendations 7 and 8 discuss strategies to enhance visibility.)

There are fewer monitors than blunters in the world, and monitors are more likely than blunters to be literate, health literate, and skilled at using the Internet. The idea of narrowing the initial focus to monitors can be disturbing to those who believe it is essential to reach the less literate groups in their communities. The reality is that less literate consumers not only have difficulty using print or Web-based reports but also are unlikely to consider looking at quality reports in gathering information. This does not mean that blunters are not motivated to get good health care for themselves and their families, just that the pathways to reaching them are different than for monitors.

It is important to make reports as easy to understand as possible for people with lower levels of education. Still, people in this group are most likely to seek information from media that do not require them to read and understand text and graphs. Such media include radio, TV, and perhaps most important, other people. To reach less literate groups, or groups that are more comfortable speaking a language other than English, the strategies presented in Recommendations 3 and 7 are essential. Promotion and dissemination efforts also should target those who can influence others because they are trusted sources of information. People ask friends and family for health care recommendations, and they can extend a report's influence. People who are highly engaged in health issues and are natural helpers are likely "early adopters" of new health information.

Heightening awareness of your reporting among this group through community organization newsletters, health-related blogs, or other media can provide an avenue into hard-to-reach groups. Keep in mind that a "trusted source" can vary by topic. For example, consumers may trust physicians for reports on clinical issues and look to health plans for information on medical groups.

Recommendation No. 3: Engage Those Who Can Help You Learn About and Reach Your Audience

Multistakeholder sponsors, such as CVEs, must strategize from the outset about how to include organizations that are knowledgeable about and trusted by their report's intended audiences. Many groups can help: Employers can help reach their employees and their families; health plans can spread the word to their members; and providers can contribute to getting out the word out to patients. However, the stakeholders that are especially important to help you learn about and reach your audience are consumer and patient advocacy groups [7]:

- Consumer advocacy organizations that serve women, children, older adults, members of minority groups, and labor members, such as:
    - AARP
    - AFL-CIO
    - NAACP
- Organizations that serve these populations, such as:

    - The Arc (the world's largest community-based organization of and for people with intellectual and developmental disabilities)
    - Area Agencies on Aging and others in the "aging network"
    - Easter Seals and other disease-specific groups
    - YWCA and YMCA
- Faith-based organizations, such as:
    - Churches
    - Mosques
    - Synagogues
- Broad-based or policy-focused organizations, such as:
    - Citizen Action
    - Consumer's Union
    - Kiwanis Club
    - League of Women Voters
    - Lion's Club
    - Literacy Council
    - Neighborhood associations

In addition to their other considerable contributions to reporting efforts, consumer-oriented organizations can be a key resource for ensuring effective report promotion and dissemination. Community groups that advocate or provide support for people with the kinds of conditions measured in specific quality reports could make a substantial contribution. Partners with special access to groups you want to reach, such as minorities, older adults, parents of young children, people who prefer speaking a language other than English, women, or consumers in rural areas, can become critical "information intermediaries" who do hands-on promotion and dissemination of reports and, in some cases, help people use and understand them. The following list of "Roles of Information Intermediaries" was adapted from a report on the subject for people on Medicare. [8]

Roles of Information

Intermediaries Promote and Disseminate Information

- Promote the availability of information, assistance, and decision support.
- Disseminate information "broadcast" through one or more channels.

- Disseminate information to particular groups of people in a more tailored and customized manner.
- Legitimate the trustworthiness and usefulness of information materials and sources of information and decision support.

Connect Specific Individuals With Information When Needed

- Identify specific individuals who need information and decision support.
- Refer people to appropriate sources of information and decision support.

Provide, Explain, and Apply Information to Specific Individuals

- Educate and inform people through person-to-person interactions.
- Help people understand and interpret comparative information.
- Help people apply information to their own circumstances.

Provide Decision Support

- Help people identify what is most important to them in choosing a health plan or provider and the constraints they face in making a choice.
- Help people on Medicare narrow the number or range of options, consistent with what is most important to them and the constraints they face.
- Recommend more desirable options, either in general or based on the individual's characteristics and preferences.

These organizations also can help conduct formal and informal audience research to identify the kind of report to use to attract those you want to reach. Reports will be more likely to resonate with the public if they address the providers people are most interested in learning about and include measures that are important and make sense to them. Clearly, these are "up front" questions. In addition, audience research can help identify modes of dissemination most likely to reach people, benefits to highlight in promoting the report, and barriers to overcome in raising awareness and achieving access, as well as what will make consumers most likely to trust the report.

When seeking to involve those with special access to your audience, you cannot start too early, especially if your intended audience is vulnerable or often ignored. If people think they are being included only after many of the important decisions have been made, they are less likely to support the efforts. They are not interested in being a rubber stamp and may be quick to think they are being used.

Also consider reasons these organizations might be persuaded to work with you. Identify the benefits for them, including but not limited to serving their constituencies well. Many have limited resources and may need some type of compensation for the time they contribute.

Finally, treat community-based, consumer-oriented organizations with respect. Value and recognize their opinions and recommendations equally to the input from stakeholders that may bring more technical expertise to the table. These organizations' expertise is different, but just as necessary for successful reporting. They know and understand the people you want to reach.

Do Not Forget About Secondary Audiences

Keep in mind that in addition to your primary consumer audience, you may have important secondary audiences. One important secondary audience is made up of those being rated, and they should receive the report before it goes public. There are two ways to share the report. In both cases, providers receive their own data and information about how they compare to other nonidentified providers and to whatever you are using as a comparator (the average, the top fifth of the score distribution, etc.) before the report goes public.

In one scenario, a hiatus, perhaps 6 months, follows provision of the initial data to providers. Then, a second round of data collection is completed, and these are the data reported to the public. This approach is particularly appropriate the first time a set of measures is presented. The hiatus allows providers to work on performance problems they are made aware of from the first round of data collection before the second round begins. Evidence indicates that this approach drives a significant focus on quality. [9]

In the second scenario, after providers receive their own data and the deidentified data of other providers, they are given an opportunity to correct any problems in the information before it is reported publicly. As noted in *Best Practices in Public Reporting No. 2*, some sponsors permit providers in these circumstances to publish their comments within the report.

Secondary audiences also exist in areas where elements of health care delivery interact. For hospital ratings, physicians constitute an important audience, since they admit patients to hospitals and refer patients to specialists who have privileges at one or a very small number of hospitals. It is not likely that physicians will change referral patterns overnight, but if some facilities perform poorly and do not improve, they may reconsider their relationships and referrals. PacifiCare Health Systems has some experience providing incentives to physicians in their network for referring to hospitals that provide higher quality care. [10]

It is also important to include physicians because patients may ask them about ratings. From interviews with physicians, we know they are interested in being informed about public reports of hospital quality prior to their release. They do not want to be blindsided if a patient asks about a recently issued report. While hospitals may be the most appropriate group to provide that prior notice to physicians, a multistakeholder collaborative could also be the source. [11]

Consult with the provider members of your venture to devise the best way to get this information out in your community. A communication committee as mentioned in Recommendation No. 1 is an ideal context for this kind of discussion. In their communications, for example, the Puget Sound Health Alliance CVE creates model materials for hospitals and physicians to use in communicating about reports to their medical staff, patients, media, and others. Your reporting efforts might provide similar support to these groups with tools, such as Frequently Asked Questions, key messages, model newsletter articles, and Web site text.

Currently, most physician reports focus on primary care doctors. In the future, however, reports on specialists may become available. Since many referrals to specialists come from other physicians, a report on specialists also should consider primary care physicians as an important secondary audience.

Recommendation No. 4: Use the Insights of Social Marketing

Social marketing is the application of business marketing principles and strategies to promote ideas, behaviors, and services that have high societal value. In contrast to commercial endeavors, which direct marketing at convincing consumers to buy a particular product or service, social marketing has been used in health care settings to promote healthy behaviors. Examples include using seatbelts, quitting smoking, and putting babies to sleep on their backs.

The purpose of publishing comparative quality reports is not to encourage consumers to choose a *particular* provider or plan. Rather, it is to influence consumer behaviors in accessing reports, looking at them long enough to make meaningful comparisons, and using the information to make a decision, or in some other related way. Keep these desired consumer behaviors in mind as you develop your social marketing strategy. This may be a different kind of objective than you are used to.

Good social marketing involves:

- Identifying the audiences you want to reach.
- Identifying the benefits of a product or service that will be important to your audience.
- Identifying when your audience may benefit most from your report.
- Identifying the barriers your audience might perceive or experience in taking the action you desire.
- Motivating your audience to take the action you desire.
- Placing or distributing your product/service/message where your audience can find it quickly and easily and in a location that reinforces their trust in its benefits.

More information on social marketing can be found on the Talking Quality Web site, supported by the Agency for Healthcare Research and Quality (http://www.talkingquality.gov).

Another central element of social marketing is developing key messages to use in promoting your report. As discussed in Recommendation No. 5, these key messages need to be repeated over and over again if you are to reach your audience. Messages should emphasize the benefits *your audience* will value most and effectively counter the barriers they are likely to perceive or experience.

As noted in *Best Practices in Public Reporting No. 2*, the public generally does not recognize that quality varies and that much health care is not of high quality. We recommend that this key message be incorporated into reports, right at the beginning. Evidence indicates that people respond better to messages that show them how to protect themselves from risks than to messages that show them how to "find the best."

Very often, however, stakeholder groups, especially those being rated, object to risk-oriented framing of promotional messages. In addition, some stakeholders want to emphasize transparency and the fact that new information is available as benefits of producing a quality report. They might want the report to be promoted as a way of learning how much better the providers in "x" community are compared to everyone else in the State or Nation. That approach may make sponsors and stakeholders feel good but is not likely to attract much attention in the short term.

The Puget Sound Health Alliance CVE found another approach to address this dilemma. They framed the CVE's *Community Checkup* report with the message that EVERYONE in the region needs to improve. Even among those with the best reputations, no one did everything right. All providers had room to improve, and all community members bear some responsibility for problems in quality. Providers must recommend the right care; patients have to follow through. Before that happens, employers need to purchase benefits from health plans that provide coverage for the recommended service. Puget Sound found that this framing of the issue reduces the extent to which providers feel blamed for things they do not control.

Developing a well-known and trusted brand identity is another important aspect of marketing. No one can create a brand overnight. If your organization sponsors reports as one of its major activities, you may want to use your organization's established brand to promote the report rather than creating an entirely new brand. As we discuss in Recommendation No. 5, until your brand is established in the minds of the public, you may need to make creative use of the brand identity of other organizations with whom you partner. Choose to go with a partner whose brand identity gives them credibility with your audience around health care issues.

RECOMMENDATION NO. 5: BE STRATEGIC ABOUT TIMING

A major challenge of promoting reports is the difficulty in knowing who will be making what kinds of health care decisions at what point in time. This is particularly true of decisions about selecting clinicians and facilities. Obvious times to promote reports are when they are launched or when important information is either added or updated. Unfortunately, only a very small percentage of your audience will be making a decision at exactly those points in time. It is important to remind audiences *frequently* about the availability of the report and how to access it. That way, when consumers find they need the information, your report will be closer to top of mind.

Public reports on quality are new to most people and require them to enact a new behavior. Other efforts to change health-related behaviors and social norms tell us that one message, delivered in one format and through one channel, is *never* enough. Your audience needs to get the message multiple times in different formats, from different sources, over extended periods of time before it even begins to sink in that the report is a resource available on demand.

Effective tobacco control efforts, for example, required persistent and inescapable cues and messages in a wide variety of trusted venues and contexts over a long period of time. Strong antismoking messages were delivered by laws that restricted tobacco purchases to those older than 18 and that banned smoking in workplaces and public venues, as well as through extensive mass media campaigns. The goal of the antismoking social marketing campaign was to change social norms around smoking.

> The goal of effective public reporting is to change social norms about how proactive consumers should be in making health care decisions.

This kind of all-encompassing marketing approach requires that promotion be a coordinated effort over time to reinforce key messages. Multistakeholder sponsors have an advantage since each partner may contribute to presenting key messages in different ways and venues to different groups.

Recommendation No. 6: Be Strategic About Positioning

Whether you are developing a print or Web-based report, or doing a mix, it is critical to consider your audience in determining where to *place* your report. Your initial audience research should identify all the places people go for health information, the kind of site or location they will most likely access, and the sites they are most likely to trust.

Consider Placement and Links When Using Web-Based Reports

If you are publishing a Web-based report, it is important to decide if you will create a new site for it or if you will place it on another site that is already widely trusted and used by the audience you want to reach. As mentioned above, if another organization has the right brand identity and will be viewed as trustworthy and objective by your audience, why not use their site?

A multistakeholder sponsor may also need to consider whether to locate its report on one of the major stakeholder's Web sites (and under its brand) or create a Web site for the collaborative effort. Before taking the latter approach, consider if one of the collaborative's partners is already known, trusted, and used by the audience. Consider also if it will cause problems within the partnership if one member is chosen to be "home" to the quality reports. Since most sponsors have created new Web sites for their reports, there has been little research to test the relative effectiveness of these strategies.

There is no doubt that it is useful to place links to your report's Web site on as many trustworthy and appropriate sites as possible. Pick sites consumers visit when dealing with a health problem or trying to make a decision. All kinds of organizations can serve this purpose, including consumer and patient advocacy groups, providers, employers, public agencies, and health plans; indeed, the full range of partners in the typical CVE and beyond. It is especially important to go back to the consumer and patient groups you engaged to learn about your audience and give them the opportunity to host a link to your report.

Whether or place links to your report on the Web sites of the organizations being rated is an issue that needs special consideration. For example, is it a good idea to link from a rated hospital's site to your report? Again, there is no clear evidence. Ideally, you would do this when all the hospitals rated are willing to allow the links, as you do not want to be perceived as being more influenced by some hospitals than by others.

It is best to get Web posting agreements *before* the ratings are out to ensure that organizations do not back out if they have relatively poor performance. In some cases, however, particularly when reports are first being made public, you may have to settle for a situation in which only some providers are willing to offer links to the report. The same approach can be taken in getting agreement from hospitals, physicians, or others to place print versions of your report, or a takeaway announcement about your Web site, in their offices and waiting areas. Like so much else in quality reporting, this requires a robust relationship with providers.

Even more fundamental, it is important to design your report so that it can be found easily by consumers searching the Web for information related to health care and health care providers. This means making sure your report includes prominent use of common search terms that your audience is likely to use. So-called "search optimization" techniques, in which Web site designers use specific terms to maximize the chances that a site will come up in a search, are an important step in the report design process.

We recommend that you optimize your Web site, testing a variety of search terms prior to rollout, to see whether your report comes up and where it appears in the list of search results. If potential users have to know the name of your organization or your report to find it, you have a problem. Ideally, your Web site should appear on the first page of results from a search, as close to the top as possible. Keep in mind that this requires use of terms that might be used by people who do not know your report exists.

In addition to reaching consumers who are looking for information about quality, you want to attract those who are seeking health information but are not necessarily thinking about quality. Embedding links on related sites will help bring users to your Web site. For example, placing links to your report on Web sites that consumers visit for health information is an effective tactic for reminding them to consider comparative quality information when they are, for example, deciding on a hospital for their surgery. Consumers seek health information more often than quality information. Some will be interested in learning about comparative quality if prompted to do so.

Be Aware of Multiple Quality Reports in a Single Community

One of the greatest challenges a sponsor faces is dueling quality reports; the situation can undermine the credibility of all the reports. The likelihood of this occurring is on the rise, as more organizations at all levels, including some commercial ventures, get involved with quality measurement, reporting, and improvement. To effectively promote your report in this context requires that consumers understand the comparative benefits of using and believing your report. You should provide evidence that shows how your report is more complete, more relevant, and more trustworthy, as well as easier to use.

Sometimes reports may have different scores on similar measures, perhaps because of variations in specification of the measure, scoring methodology, or time period covered. This is especially confusing to the public and irksome to those rated. Before releasing a report, make sure to examine existing reports and compare findings. You will have to make an extra effort to explain the reasons for any variation both within the report and in your interactions with the community.

Other times, reports cover different measures, e.g., one reports on one aspect of quality, such as patient safety, while another reports on patient experience for an identical or similar set of providers. The best strategy in this circumstance is to work toward a collaboration in which, at least as a first step, each report references the other, perhaps links to the other, and explains that the user would be wise to look at both reports. This is not a perfect solution, as many people will be unwilling to work at integrating information from two reports. Ultimately, a fully integrated approach to quality reporting is the best solution, but this will take time, skillful negotiation, and trust among the sponsors involved.

Recommendation No. 7: Actively Work with Media to Promote The Report

Begin early to plan how you will work with the media—both print and electronic—to promote your comparative quality report. Most sponsors typically issue a press release and hold a news conference. These steps are necessary but clearly not sufficient to yield the breadth, depth, and quality of coverage needed to raise awareness about your report.

As with other partners, start building relationships with the media as soon as possible. Identify the reporters who cover health care in the most widely trusted media in your market. Identify the radio and TV programs—particularly local programs—that address health issues. Seek out bloggers who write about health care. You need to let them know what you are doing ahead of time and give them opportunities to watch events unfold. When your data are available, you can also arrange a meeting with media representatives, individually or as a group, to preview the results and, more important, make sure they really understand what they mean.

The media want stories that will help them sell papers or get audience share and, thus, advertising revenues. The electronic media, in particular, need stories that work as "9-second sound bites." Just as it is necessary to grab the attention of consumers immediately in a report on comparative quality, it is also imperative to get to the point of your story quickly. This means you need to shape your pitch to the media as "new news."

But what is news? It has been said that "victims, villains, and simple solutions" are what make news. A horror story about a patient's terrible experience with a particular hospital is more likely to be reported than a story about the release of a report on hospital quality. It is necessary to explain the "quality story" to members of the media and entice them to cover it. In this way, you may complement social marketing efforts with what is called media advocacy or earned media by turning your messages into news. This gets them on air or in print without your having to pay advertising fees.

This approach has served key health behavior efforts extremely well. Your goal is to place periodic stories—news and features—about your quality report. Some people think the public will respond better to your story as earned media than as paid advertising because when you advertise, it is clear you are shaping your message.

The challenge is to identify interesting and surprising findings in your report as "teasers" to interest the media without "victimizing" or "villainizing" anyone. Focusing on your data, pitch stories to the media that:

- Compare your community to others.
- Reveal trends as your reports are updated.
- Report on improvements in quality over time and how they were achieved.

In addition to talking about report content, you also might interest the media and the public in stories about how disparate health care stakeholders reached decisions on tough issues, how individual patients and consumers benefited from using your reports, or how someone fared who wished they had used your report. A personal story will always be of greater interest than something that is abstract and general.

Craft Policies to Ensure Consistent Messaging

It is important to develop guidelines for interactions with the media, particularly for multistakeholder groups. Everyone must be on the same page and use the same key messages. Identify who the primary media contacts will be and make sure they coordinate efforts, not only at the outset but also on an ongoing basis. Keep in mind our earlier suggestions to create a communication committee and take advantage of the expertise that lives within your partner organizations. Expertise in media relations, while growing in public and nonprofit organizations, may be more established in private sector organizations, such as employers.

Consider also whether rated entities may be allowed to use selected extracts of the report in their advertising. In one of the early CAHPS® (Consumer Assessment of Healthcare Providers and Systems) demonstrations in Oregon, rated health plans signed agreements that prohibited this. They were not permitted to publish their own ratings without the comparisons; they also could not advertise the measures on which they did well and leave out those on which they did poorly.

A current example of one approach to this issue comes from the National Committee for Quality Assurance (NCQA). NCQA has issued policy guidelines that must be followed by any organization (health plan, hospital, physician practice) it accredits or recognizes in one of its programs. For example, organizations may use only the most recent results and cannot claim to be accredited or recognized unless the process is complete. [12]

RECOMMENDATION NO. 8: USE ADVERTISING TO PROMOTE THE REPORT

Although we have noted the advantages of using earned media to promote reports, do not ignore paid advertising. Those who doubt their ability to interest the news media will need to depend heavily on ads. Advertising can reach broad populations, as well as target specific populations by focusing on channels and media different segments use and trust. Reach distinct cultural, regional, or age-specific audiences through newspapers, free magazines, radio spots, and TV stations.

With Web-based reports, consider advertising on the Internet to get your message out. It is possible to purchase the rights for your site to appear at the top of the list on searches involving specified key terms. Consider also buying ads on popular commercial sites (in addition to links on your partners' Web sites). Little is known about the effectiveness of Web advertising techniques for comparative quality reports. Consult Web advertising experts to define strategies that might work best given your circumstances and budget. However, here is a summary of one effort to study the impact of different kinds of advertising and promotion for a report on hospitals.

Recommendation No. 9: Use Outreach to Promote the Report and Facilitate Its Use

Outreach in this context refers to working with and through other organizations who have an ongoing relationship with one or more of your target audiences to help deliver your message. Outreach is an essential complement to media coverage and advertising in any promotion and dissemination strategy. As noted earlier, it is critical to build and sustain relationships with those who, in the natural course of daily life, interact with your audience. There are dozens of such organizations, large and small, public and private, nonprofit, and affiliated with churches and other religious organizations. Recommendation 3 has an illustrative list of such organizations.

Promoting CalHospitalCompare.org

The California HealthCare Foundation (CHCF) has spent years supporting efforts to provide hospital quality information to Californians. In 2008, CHCF reported on its study of how consumers use the Internet to manage their health care. [2,13] CHCF found that in 2007, 23 percent of those surveyed had seen hospital rating information, but only 4 percent of those had considered a change in hospital choice, and only 1 percent made a change based on the ratings.

CHCF's analysis of usage statistics from its CalHospitalCompare Web site revealed a substantial number of visits. But because about half of the traffic came from visitors who had "bookmarked" the site on their Internet browsers, it was believed that industry insiders were responsible for as much traffic as consumers. In response, CHCF launched a campaign to increase consumer awareness of its Web site, hoping to drive more consumers to the site and increase their use of the data in hospital choice decisions. (Note that hospital participation in this initiative was voluntary; CHCF demonstrated the benefits of their participation by showing them that consumers visited the hospitals' Web sites as well as CalHospital Compare.org.)

Most report sponsors do not have the resources that CHCF had to launch its awareness campaign and track the cost-effectiveness of different promotion and advertising strategies. The campaign focused on maternity care—a "shoppable" condition—targeting expectant mothers in the San Francisco Bay Area as a distinct media market.

The aim was to tap into mothers' desires for information and to reassure them that CalHospitalCompare's ratings were unbiased and independent. It was primarily an online campaign, which used a strategy of placing display and text ads on local news Web sites, community participation sites, and online networks such as Google and Yahoo. CHCF purchased keywords from search engines, including the names of Bay Area hospitals, the term "hospital reviews," and terms relevant to maternity and pregnancy, such as "C-Section" and "NICU." The campaign also employed branded e-mail messages and event sponsorships.

What worked? What didn't? What was cost-effective? The campaign's display ads led to more than 14 million "impressions," or page views by individuals, and 12,000-plus new "clicks," or visits, to the CalHospitalCompare Web site. Selected search terms resulted in fewer impressions, only 1.3 million, but to more clicks, more than 13,000. Branded e-mails were not nearly as effective, resulting in 10,000 impressions and only 100 clicks. The awareness campaign succeeded in driving traffic at the Web sites of Bay Area hospitals. Indeed, page views during the campaign were six times higher than average page views of major hospitals elsewhere in the State.

Placement mattered also. Costs for online ads are based on "per million impressions" or the number of "clicks" that result from the ads. The cost for both of these actions was lowest for ads placed on search engine sites and much higher for ads on the Web sites of local newspapers. The ads most successful in generating traffic at CalHospitalCompare focused on C-Section rates at different hospitals and on "finding the hospital that is best for you." Ads that were less direct—such as those that spoke about how one typically gets more help choosing baby names than in picking a hospital—were less successful.

CHCF's campaign provides rare evidence of how to successfully build an audience for a comparative quality report, and how to encourage hospitals to collaborate in the reporting effort, as well as which promotional methods are most effective.

For multistakeholder groups, partners are key. Employers can help reach workers and their families; labor unions can help reach their members; and providers (hospitals, physicians, community health clinics) can help reach their patients. Public agencies can help reach those they serve, whether these are people with Medicaid coverage or people who use public health services;

condition-specific advocacy groups can help reach specific groups of patients and their caregivers; and so on.

Tap Existing Networks

It is likely that you will need to reach beyond your partners to gain the widest possible awareness of your report. To reach seniors, for example, take advantage of State AARP chapters along with what is called the "aging network," the vast array of primarily small- or medium-size agencies that serve the social and health needs of elders. In many communities—especially those of color—faith-based organizations can be of great assistance. Social clubs and service clubs exist for all kinds of cultural groups in your community. This is where people congregate, where they chat, and where they expect to get information that is in their best interest.

Educational institutions are natural partners; this does not just mean elementary and high schools, but also community colleges, adult education programs (including those who provide classes in English as a Second Language), daycare centers, and after school programs. Programs directed toward children provide a great way to reach out to parents, especially if your report includes measures of health care for children.

The impact that effective outreach can have is exemplified by the outreach efforts made when the State Children's Health Insurance Program (SCHIP) began more than 10 years ago. States eager to enroll as many eligible children as possible used the full range of organizations discussed above and more to get out the word about the then-new program. Those who did more outreach enrolled more children. [14,15]

When reaching out to these groups, it is critical to demonstrate that you have no "ax to grind" and that your report is not a form of advertising for any particular insurance company or medical provider. Similarly, you must show how the organizations and their members will benefit from working with you. Work collaboratively with these organizations to identify the best tools for reaching their constituencies. And do not be surprised if they propose face-to-face contact instead of, or in addition to, the use of pamphlets, brochures, posters, and other written materials. They also will want materials that are user friendly. Indeed, staff of community-based organizations may be an excellent source of feedback on your report; if they do not find it compelling, relevant, and easy to understand and navigate, chances are their constituencies will not either.

Do Not Forget Libraries

Last, but by no means least, public libraries offer important promotion and dissemination opportunities. Libraries are all about access to information, and most libraries today realize that a significant part of their service to the public is to help those caught in the digital divide gain access to both print and Web-based information. At least two CVEs have experience working with libraries for this purpose: Puget Sound Health Alliance and Pittsburgh Regional Health Initiative.

Recommendation No. 10: Gather and Analyze Feedback on the Report and Its Promotion

Given the investment of time and effort in a public report, sponsors should have a mechanism to assess its impact. Knowing how many people a report reaches, whom it reaches, and how it is received and used will be helpful in refining future versions. Simply tracking online "hits" offers a rough gauge of use of Web-based reports. It also is possible to track more detailed information, such as pages viewed, time spent per page, and links that produce the most traffic. Many sponsors of Web-based reports take advantage of the extensive free tracking and analysis services available. However, to understand how people respond to and use the Web site, other methods are needed.

A survey built into the Web site is one possible feedback mechanism. Focus groups with key audiences will provide information about how well the report meets the needs of those subgroups. Community partners, such as employers, payers, and community organizations, may help by recruiting their members to participate in focus groups. Conducting two to four focus groups involving five to 12 participants each can yield a great deal of useful information.

Similarly, some community partners, such as employers or unions, want indepth information about their employees or members. In surveying their employees or members, they may be willing to include questions about awareness, use, and perceived value of the comparative quality report. These kinds of efforts may contribute to your overall assessment and provide insights for improvement.

Sponsors may seek to learn how easy or difficult it is to use their Web site, as well as inquire about what consumers find useful or not useful and what kind of additional information they would be interested in seeing in future reports. Information about how users heard about the report will help sponsors refine efforts to attract new users to the Web site. Similarly, quotes from users in focus groups and interviews may be useful to include in the promotion materials for future releases of the report. Finally, tracking media coverage of the report will indicate the level of public awareness, as well as help sponsors understand how the report is being portrayed to the public.

PURPOSE OF REPORT SERIES

The purpose of this three-part series of reports is to provide practical approaches to designing public reports that make health care performance information clear, meaningful, and usable by consumers. The goal is to help sponsors present information so that a wide variety of people can understand and apply it easily to key decisions, even if they do not want to spend a lot of time on details and have limited technical knowledge of the subject.

Together the three reports cover the wide range of issues and challenges faced by report sponsors:

- *Best Practices in Public Reporting No. 1: How To Effectively Present Health Care Performance Data to Consumers* focuses on the challenges involved in designing a public report card so that the performance information is easily understood by consumers and on strategies to make it easier for consumers to understand and use comparative health care quality reports.
- *Best Practices in Public Reporting No. 2: Maximizing Consumer Understanding of Public Comparative Quality Reports: Effective Use of Explanatory Information* focuses on the explanatory information in public reports, beyond the performance data itself, that helps to accurately communicate quality ratings to consumers and motivate them to use the ratings in making informed health care decisions.
- *Best Practices in Public Reporting No. 3: How To Maximize Public Awareness and Use of Comparative Quality Reports Through Effective Promotion and Dissemination Strategies* applies social marketing and other principles to explore how to target reports to specific audiences,

develop messages to promote the report with key audiences, engage consumer advocacy and community groups in promoting reports and helping people use them, disseminate reports through trusted channels, and ensure that consumers see and use comparative quality reports.

REFERENCES

[1] 2008 Update on consumers' views of patient safety and quality information. Menlo Park, CA: *Kaiser Family Foundation*; October 15, 2008.

[2] Harris Interactive. Just looking: consumer use of the Internet to manage care. Oakland: *California HealthCare Foundation*; May 2008.

[3] Hibbard JH, Stockard J, Tusler M. The long-term effect of public performance reporting on hospital quality improvement, market share, and reputation: evidence from a controlled experiment. Health Aff 2005 Jul/Aug;24(4):1150-60.

[4] Hibbard JH, Stockard J, Tusler M. It isn't just about choice: the potential of a public performance report to affect the public image of hospitals. *Med. Care Res. Rev.* 2005 Jun;62(3):358-71.

[5] Miller SM. Monitoring and blunting: validation of a questionnaire to assess styles of information-seeking under threat. *J. Pers. Soc. Psychol.* 1987 Feb;52:345-53.

[6] Miller SM. Monitoring versus blunting styles of coping with cancer influence the information patients want and need about their disease. Implications for cancer screening and management. *Cancer* 1995 Jul 15;76:167-77.

[7] Sweeney, J. The Community Quality Collaborative leader's guide to engaging consumers. Rockville, MD: Agency for Healthcare Research and Quality; November 2008. Available at: http://www.ahrq.gov/QUAL/value/caguide.htm.

[8] Sofaer S. A classification scheme of individuals and agencies who serve as information intermediaries for people on Medicare. Report to the Center for Beneficiary Services. Baltimore, MD: *Health Care Financing Administration*; May 2000.

[9] Barr JK, Boni CE, Kochurcka KA, et al. Public reporting of hospital patient satisfaction: the Rhode Island experience. *Health Care Financ. Rev.* 2002;23(4):51-70.

[10] Rosenthal MB, Frank RG, Li Z, et al. Early experience With pay-for-performance: from concept to practice. *JAMA* 2005;294:1788-93.
[11] Barr J, Bernard SL, Sofaer S, et al. Physicians' views on public reporting of hospital quality data. *Med. Care Res. Rev.* 2008;65(6):655-73.
[12] Guidelines for marketing and advertising: NCQA 2008 physician and hospital quality certification. Washington, DC: National Committee for Quality Assurance; October 2008. Available at: http://www.ncqa.org/Portals/0/Marketing/AdGuidelines/PHQCertification_12_23_08.pdf
[13] Shannon M. CalHospitalCompare.org San Francisco maternity campaign. CAHPS-SOPS User Group Meeting, Joint CAHPS Session on Public Reporting: "Engaging Consumers in Using Quality Reports: What it Takes To Capture Eyeballs; 2008 Dec; Scottsdale, Arizona.
[14] Felland L, Benoit AM. Communities play key role in extending public health insurance to children. *Issue Brief Cent Stud. Health Syst. Change* 2001 Oct;(44):1-4.
[15] Kincheloe J, Frates J, Brown ER. Determinants of children's participation in California's Medicaid and SCHIP programs. *Health Serv. Res.* 2006 Aug 17;42(2):847-66.

In: Public Reporting of Health Care ... ISBN: 978-1-63482-346-3
Editor: Alexis Pratt © 2015 Nova Science Publishers, Inc.

Chapter 4

QUALITY REPORTING ON MEDICARE'S COMPARE SITES: LESSONS LEARNED FROM CONSUMER RESEARCH, 2001-2013*

Margaret Gerteis, Cicely Thomas, Lauren Blatt, Sally Crelia, Alyson Marano Ward, Kelly Moriarty, Monica Sarmiento, Myra Tanamor and Russ Tisinger

I. INTRODUCTION

Public Reporting on Medicare.Gov

The Centers for Medicare & Medicaid Services (CMS) has been the driving force behind public reporting on health plan and provider performance in the United States for more than a decade. Based on the premise that making performance information available to the public will lead to a more rational health care marketplace, Medicare's *Compare* web tools were designed initially as sites for consumers to find and compare the performance of health plans, physicians, hospitals, home health agencies, nursing homes, and dialysis facilities. The Patient Protection and Affordable Care Act (ACA) of 2010 now

* This is an edited, reformatted and augmented version of a report prepared under contract with L&M Policy Research and Mathematica Policy Research for the Centers for Medicare & Medicaid Services which issued the report September 2014.

directs CMS to further refine and enhance efforts to educate consumers about quality and empower them to manage their health care.

Over the years, CMS has begun to change its stance on public reporting, from a policy of posting data without interpretation to recognizing that consumers need at least some interpretative guidance (even if only to say whether higher or lower numbers are better). As the volume of publicly reported information grows, CMS is also beginning to support the idea of summarizing and synthesizing information through composites and symbols, acknowledging that consumers' ability to process page after page of statistics and bar graphs is limited.

However, the lay public is not the only intended audience. Public reporting is, increasingly, a vehicle for making performance information available to different constituencies for different purposes, and the *Compare* sites are also now the designated channels for publicly reporting performance information related to federal initiatives, including incentive payment programs for value-based purchasing, provider participation in quality-reporting registries, use of health information technology, and measures of resource use. This expanding mandate complicates the task of conveying information to consumers. Statutory time lines can leave little time to consider what the implications or underlying messages are for lay users of the *Compare* tools, or to design new website content and displays for a consumer audience.

Since CMS first began planning its quality initiatives and public reporting agenda nearly 15 years ago, the authors of this report have researched quality reporting issues from a consumer perspective under a number of contracts with CMS — from early formative research on consumers' information-seeking behavior, decision-making scenarios, and target audiences, to the development and testing of prototype *Compare* tools, cognitive testing of new measures and displays, and research on alternative reporting formats and organizational frameworks.

This report draws on that body of research. What differentiates this work from that of consumer researchers and consultants operating in other venues is our specific focus on CMS's quality initiatives and *Compare* tools and the constraints of public reporting in that context. We recognize that CMS's decisions are informed not just by consumer research, but also by policy judgments and politics, by technological and financial limitations, and by competing stakeholder interests — issues that will always be in play. Our objective, then, is not to create a primer for public reporting (which already exist[1]), or to make specific recommendations that may or may not be feasible to implement. Rather, our aim is to offer some insights, based on what we have learned, about the interplay of factors that shape consumers' perceptions and ability to engage with publicly reported information. These issues, too, must be taken into account in the ongoing development of CMS's *Compare* tools.

A Social Marketing Approach to Consumer Research

Since we first began working with CMS to help design and promote its quality-reporting initiatives and *Compare* websites, social marketing principles have provided the framework for our consumer research. The "four P's" of marketing emphasize the design of a *product* that meets an identified need for an identified consumer segment, made available in a *place* that is accessible to consumers when they need it, at a *price* they are willing to pay, and product *promotion* that uses the right messaging to convey this information to the right audience. Social marketing applies these principles to the development and promotion of products designed to serve a social purpose, rather than for commercial gain. In this case, the social purpose, broadly speaking, is to improve the quality of health care and to engage consumers in using publicly reported information to that end.

Within the constraints of CMS's developmental time lines and budgets for the quality initiatives and web tools, the research supporting this work has followed a defined arc, beginning with formative research to understand who the consumers are and the context in which they make their decisions — what factors enter into their choices, who and what influence them, what constraints they face. This is the first step in defining the primary audience for publicly reported information, as well as secondary audiences who influence their actions or decisions. To this end, much of the early work we undertook with CMS explored consumers' information-seeking and decision-making behavior under different scenarios — focusing first on planning for post-acute or long-term care (in nursing homes or home health settings) to inform CMS's Nursing Home and Home Health Quality Initiatives and focusing later on acute care in hospital settings to support the development of *Hospital Compare*.[2] This work relied heavily on small group discussions with patients and caregivers, health care providers, and professionals who serve as information intermediaries for consumers.

Once the context of decision making is better understood, the research focus shifts to product design, product positioning, and messaging — that is, the design of the *Compare* tools, themselves. For this work, we have more often used one-on-one, in-depth interviews with primary or secondary consumer audiences, both to develop the content and format of the tools and to test their usability. Because the price or "cost" of the product, in this case, is related to the cognitive burden of using the information, we have used cognitive testing techniques to determine how readily and accurately consumers can understand and interpret narrative content and data displays in different formats. We have used this approach both to inform the initial development of the *Compare* tools and to test ways to incorporate changes and additions, as new measures of quality and efficiency are added.

Although much of our focus has been on formative research, product development, and refinement, we have also explored ways to get publicly reported information into consumers' hands at key points in the decision-making process, as well as the potential use of decision aids, checklists, and other tools to make the information more usable. For example, when research on post-acute care placement decisions shed light on the central role that hospital discharge planners play, we explored the feasibility of using these professionals as intermediaries to disseminate information on the quality performance of nursing homes or home health agencies to consumers. Our early research on nursing home placement decisions also revealed that although family caregivers wanted to visit a nursing home before placing a family member there, they did not know what to look for or what questions to ask. We therefore developed and tested a checklist that would link the publicly reported quality data for a given nursing home to observable practices or questions to ask.

Social Marketing

Social Marketing applies the principles of product marketing, often described in terms of the "four P's," to the advancement of social agendas:

- PRODUCT: Does the product (the publicly reported health services information) meet consumers' needs?
- PLACE: Is the health services information accessible to consumers when and where they need it?
- PRICE: Is the cost of the product (the time and effort it takes to access the information) worth the benefit to consumers?
- PROMOTION: How can consumers learn about the information on the CMS website?

As suggested above, the research methodologies we have used have varied somewhat, depending on the purpose of the task at hand and the audience of interest. Research in a new topic area typically begins with a review of the research literature and an environmental scan. This may include reviewing existing research on health care communication, risk communication, decision making, health literacy, and other factors, as well as public reporting practices in other venues. Key informant interviews help the research team better understand the rationale and context for reporting specific measures or measurement methodologies. Reviewing research questions and methods with groups of stakeholders can provide additional insights and perspectives. Direct observation can also be a useful qualitative research technique — for example, shadowing hospital discharge planners during the workday to better understand the environment and context in which post-acute care placement decisions are made.

For primary research with consumers, family caregivers, health care providers, and other professionals, we have most often used two common qualitative research methodologies — focus groups and in-depth interviews — each of which has its uses and limitations:

- *Focus Groups* are facilitated group discussions appropriate for exploring values, attitudes, perceptions, and behaviors based on participants' shared characteristics or common experiences, and are particularly useful in formative research. Because group dynamics can obscure important differences among individual group members, however, we have found focus groups to be less effective in product development or usability testing with consumers. Moreover, focus groups may not work well for physicians, whose need to establish their authority in a group of peers can preclude productive give-and-take discussion.
- *One-On-One Interview Methodologies* are more appropriate for in-depth exploration of individual attitudes and experiences or potentially sensitive topics; cognitive testing of users' understanding and interpretation of information; and usability testing to observe how individuals navigate a particular web tool, what features they use (or miss), and how they accomplish particular tasks. As noted above, one-on-one interviews are also the best method for eliciting information about the perceptions and experiences of physicians or other professionals who may feel the need to compete in focus group settings. However, one-on-one interviews do not allow researchers to

observe how participants would interact with others around a particular topic or piece of information.
- *Dyads* (groupings of two research participants with one interviewer) offer a useful alternative to one-on-one interviews, in some cases — for example, when exploring the role of family caregivers or other intermediaries on consumers' understanding of information.

Regardless of the methodology, the aim always is to recruit research participants from the community who are broadly representative of the target audience of interest. In most cases, we have found that this is best accomplished by using community-based market research firms to handle recruitment, using screening protocols developed by the research team to achieve the desired participant mix. Relying on referrals from professionals or community-based organizations may yield a more skewed participant sample, we have found, although it may be necessary in some circumstances.

Research Objectives for Medicare's Compare Tools

- *Identifying Target Groups And Target Audiences*, the people whose behavior you aim to influence (or those who influence them).
- *Conducting Formative Research* to understand target audience needs, perceptions, and behaviors.
- *Developing Communication Strategies* to reach these audiences and influence their behavior.
- *Developing Products*, and testing and refining them to tailor messaging and content to the strategies of the communication campaign.
- *Testing Usability*, to determine whether, and how readily, the product can be used.

Lessons Learned from Consumer Research

Most of the consumer research that the authors (and other researchers in the field) have conducted in recent years has focused on presenting comparative performance data to the lay public in ways that will inform their choice of health care plans or providers. However, there is scant evidence to suggest that consumers consult or use such information for this purpose[3] — in part, because other issues loom larger in their personal decisions, in part because the performance information currently reported may not seem relevant to the decisions they face, and in part because they may not know such information exists. Informing consumer choice implies a focus on the individual and would require tailoring information to the specific decisions that individuals face, in practice.

With these considerations in mind, our research team has also begun to take a somewhat different tack in our approach to consumer research, framing discussions around questions about health care quality and perceived variations in quality, rather than around issues of choice, per se. This approach is based on the idea, supported by some evidence,[4] that public reporting can stimulate improvements in quality and efficiency through mechanisms other than consumer choice. The objective (and challenge), in this case, is to engage consumers in thinking about health care quality and efficiency at a conceptual level that may or may not bear directly on the individual choices they face.

In this report, we synthesize key findings from both lines of inquiry. In Section II, we begin by summarizing what we have learned about consumer decision making under different circumstances. In Section III, we highlight similarities and differences between consumers' and professionals' understanding of quality and efficiency in health care. In Section IV, we discuss the specific challenges of conveying clear, accurate, and usable performance information to consumers. In Section V, we present some of the common issues related to website navigation and usability that we have encountered.

Our aim is not to document in detail everything we have learned over the years, but to highlight the most prominent and consistent themes that seem to us most relevant to engaging consumers in questions about health care quality and efficiency. Nor do we seek to synthesize the work of other researchers in this field, although we regularly review this literature as part of our ongoing work. Unless otherwise noted, the observations offered here are based only on our own work.

Assumptions Underlying "Informed Choice"

- Consumers are the decision makers.
- Consumers have a choice.
- Consumers perceive consequences to their choices.
- Publicly reported information is understandable to consumers and relevant to their perceived needs.

- Consumers see publicly reported information as reflecting meaningful differences in performance.

II. Understanding the Context of Consumers' Choices and Decisions

One of the central premises of public reporting has been that comparative data on performance will lead to better quality and efficiency by informing consumer choice in a competitive marketplace. This assumes that consumers are the decision makers, have choices, perceive consequences to those choices, and can see meaningful differences in performance that are relevant to their decisions.

In practice, however, this may not be the case. In this chapter, we review common scenarios around decisions about selecting health plans and the types of providers included in each of Medicare's *Compare* tools, in light of assumptions underlying informed choice.

Understanding the Decision Process

- What is the context for the decision?
- What information do consumers look for or need?
- Who makes the decision?
- How much choice do they have?
- How does timing affect their ability to weigh choices?

Selecting a Health Plan

What is the context for the decision?	• Consumers tend to look for a health plan only if they need to. If they already have a plan, they might not be motivated to review their options or take action unless there is some change in their life circumstances (for example, a move or a change in employment, health, financial, or marital status).
What information do consumers look for or need?	• Consumers look for information relevant to their particular needs and circumstances, including specific benefits and covered services, provider

	networks, out-of-pocket costs (for premiums and co-pays), and prescription drug coverage.
Who makes the decision?	• Consumers are usually the primary decision makers, but their decisions may be influenced by others (such as family members, friends, counselors). Formal and informal information intermediaries (such as State Health Insurance Assistance Program counselors) may also play a role.
How much choice do they have?	• All Medicare beneficiaries have some options, although choices may be limited by personal circumstances.
How does timing affect their ability to weigh choices?	• The timing of decisions, linked to eligibility or open-enrollment periods, is usually sufficient to allow consumers to gather, review, and compare information about health plan characteristics and performance to inform their decisions.

Selecting a Physician

What is the context for the decision?	• Circumstances surrounding a search for a physician vary, but may be affected by a change in patient's life circumstances (for example, a move, change in health insurance, or a new health concern), a physician's move or retirement, or a patient's dissatisfaction with an existing physician.
What information do consumers look for or need?	• Consumers consider other physicians or health professionals, friends, and family members to be the most trusted sources of information about physicians. • They may also look for information about a physician's credentials and specialized training or experience; hospital affiliation; personal characteristics (including gender, race or ethnicity, primary language spoken); proximity; participation in the patient's insurance plan; and availability.

Who makes the decision?	• Consumers (or their family members) usually select their own primary care physicians. • Primary care or other physicians usually refer patients to specialists, although consumers may sometimes seek out specialists on their own (for example, for a second opinion).
How much choice do they have?	• Choices of both primary care and specialist physicians may be limited to the provider network covered by the consumer's health plan, or by providers' willingness to accept the patient's insurance. • Choices will also be limited by the supply of physicians available in a given specialty in a particular geographic market.
How does timing affect their ability to weigh choices?	• Timing will vary with circumstances, depending on the urgency of the need.

Selecting a Hospital

What is the context for the decision?	• Except in emergency situations or for childbirth, patients typically do not select the hospital. They go to the hospital to which their doctor refers them. • Under emergency circumstances, consumers choose hospitals based on proximity, reputation, prior experience, or their doctor's recommendation.
What information do consumers look for or need?	• For emergencies, consumers are interested in information about wait times. • For non-emergency admissions, consumers are most interested in information about the hospital's (and physician's) track record in treating their condition. • Consumers may also be interested in physician and other staff credentials, staffing ratios, and a hospital's recognized areas of expertise ("centers of excellence").

Who makes the decision?	• In emergency situations, patients, their friends or family members, or emergency medical personnel make decisions about which hospital to use. • In non-emergency situations, the choice of hospital is usually determined by the patient's doctor.
How much choice do they have?	• Hospital choice may also be limited by insurance coverage or the availability of needed specialized services, as well as the number and types of hospitals in the geographic market.
How does timing affect their ability to weigh choices?	• There is no time to weigh information and make deliberative choices in most emergency situations. • For childbirth or elective hospital admissions, patients and their family members may have the time and motivation to consider options and engage in informed decision making.

Arranging Home Health Services

What is the context for the decision?	• Most consumers understand very little about Medicare-covered home health services. They think in terms of the therapist or nurse who will come to see them, rather than the agency that will send them.
What information do consumers look for or need?	• Patients and families need to know what specific services Medicare will and will not cover. They also need to know what services will be provided and how often and for how long they will be provided.
Who makes the decision?	• Most patients have no practical sense about what to look for in a home health agency. They willingly defer to the discharge planner's (or doctor's) judgment, unless they have a preference based on prior experience. • Arrangements for post-acute home health care are almost always made by hospital discharge planners, case managers, or physicians.

How much choice do they have?	• Although Medicare may require that patients be offered more than one agency to choose from, available options will be limited to agencies in the patient's geographic area that have the resources to provide the specific services needed when those services are required. • The availability of home health services and competition in home health markets also varies widely in different geographic regions.
How does timing affect their ability to weigh choices?	• Patients who have some scheduled procedures (such as orthopedic surgery) may know in advance that post-acute home health care will be required, and discharge planning might begin early. • However, arrangements for home health care are often made within a few hours of a patient's discharge, leaving little time for consumers to weigh options. • Hospital discharge planners are most interested in an agency's ability to provide timely and reliable care (especially for difficult cases), because they want to expedite a patient's discharge and prevent short-term readmission.

Nursing Home Placements

What is the context for the decision?	• Decisions about nursing home placements are usually precipitated by a medical crisis, when emotions are running high. • Nursing homes have a negative connotation, and consumers worry about problems with quality and safety. • Family members may have a strong cultural aversion to the idea of placing a sick and elderly relative in a nursing home.
What information do consumers look for or need?	• Consumers express interest in information about staffing ratios and safety inspections. • They may resist performance information based

	on negative outcomes, however, because it reinforces their fears.
Who makes the decision?	• Decisions about post-acute, short-term, or long-term nursing home placements are almost always made by patients' family members, in consultation with hospital discharge planners, case managers, or physicians.
How much choice do they have?	• Options will be limited by the availability of beds and services at the appropriate level of care, family finances or insurance coverage, and market characteristics.
How does timing affect their ability to weigh choices?	• Most family members resist thinking about the potential need for a nursing home placement or other long-term care until circumstances compel them to do so. • Nursing home placement decisions typically take place within a few days of a pending discharge from a hospital stay, which may leave little time to explore options.

Choosing a Dialysis Facility

What is the context for the decision?	• Patients with end-stage renal disease may have little understanding of what dialysis will entail, or what to look for, until they have experienced it. • After they have been on dialysis for a while, patients are better able to understand, process, and consider comparative information on facility performance, and plan accordingly.
What information do consumers look for or need?	• Factors important to patients in choosing a facility initially include physician (nephrologist) affiliation; proximity to home or work and/or access to transportation; space availability and convenience of hours of operation; comfort and amenities; and cleanliness. • Unlike consumers facing most other choice

	decisions, patients who have had a long-term relationship with a dialysis facility have a deeper understanding of clinical processes of care and the associated measures of performance.
Who makes the decision?	• Patients with end-stage renal disease must select an outpatient facility for their ongoing dialysis care. Physicians (nephrologists), hospital discharge planners, or case managers may assist with initial placement decisions.
How much choice do they have?	• Available options will be limited by the number of facilities that have space available, are accessible to the patient, and have the capacity to provide the specific services required (hemodialysis, peritoneal dialysis, home dialysis instruction, home dialysis). • Facilities might also refuse to accept patients who have failed to keep scheduled appointments in the past.
How does timing affect their ability to weigh choices?	• Patients with chronic kidney disease may know in advance that they will require dialysis and be able to plan ahead, in collaboration with physicians or case managers. • However, many patients might be unaware, or in denial, until they are in crisis and require dialysis urgently.

In sum, the circumstances surrounding the kinds of health care decisions *Medicare's Compare* tools are intended to inform vary markedly, and the assumptions underlying the concept of informed choice may not hold true. Patients may not be the primary decision makers, their choices may be limited, and their informational needs are likely to be idiosyncratic, depending on their individual circumstances. They may have neither the time nor the motivation to weigh options.

Consumers choose the physicians with whom they have an ongoing relationship, and they look for health plans that include those doctors in their network. But their doctors are most often the ones who decide which specialists their patients should use; specialists determine which hospitals patients will be treated at; and hospitals make the arrangements for patients' post-acute home health or skilled nursing care.

Developing social marketing strategies for publicly reported information on quality and efficiency to influence provider choice thus requires recognizing how health care decisions are made, in practice, and the central role that doctors, family members, and hospital personnel play in the decision process.

Decision Making in Practice

- Consumers may or may not be the primary decision makers.
- Choices are often limited.
- Circumstances may or may not leave time for consumers to weigh options.
- Informational needs are highly specific to individual circumstances.

III. Professionals' vs. Consumers' Understanding of Quality and Efficiency

In real life, consumers look for information relevant to their personal circumstances, when making decisions about health plans or providers: Does this health plan cover the specific services I need? Does this doctor know how to treat my condition? Does this provider accept my insurance? Which hospital is my doctor affiliated with? Does the doctor or staff speak my language? Is there a nursing home close by that has a bed for my mother? If this is the kind of information consumers are looking for, how, if at all, do questions about quality or efficiency enter into the equation, and what do consumers make of the kind of information presented on the *Compare* sites?

In this chapter, we look at the differences between professionals' and consumers' perceptions and the practical implications of these differences. We begin by reviewing the professional thinking that has shaped public reporting on the *Compare* sites (and elsewhere), and consumers' take on reported quality measures. We then look more closely at how consumers themselves understand quality and efficiency in health care, and the factors that shape their perceptions. Finally, we review formative research into the development of a common framework that can bridge the gap to engage consumers in thinking about health care quality and efficiency at a broader level.

Measuring and Reporting on Quality and Efficiency: The Professional Perspective

Although the *Compare* sites are ostensibly designed for consumers, the important decisions about what to measure, how to measure it, and how to report it are made by quality professionals and health care providers operating within a professional framework of quality oversight or quality improvement. This orientation entails a focus on the identifiable *problems* in health care delivery — standards of care that are not uniformly adhered to, areas of performance where there are noteworthy variations. Among professionals operating in this context, a fair degree of consensus has evolved about the criteria that quality measures should meet before being adopted for large-scale monitoring or reporting initiatives: they should address important aspects of care that health care providers can control, be firmly grounded in evidence-based standards of care, and be capable of detecting meaningful differences in performance using data that are readily available.[5]

This professional quality perspective has, in turn, shaped what is reported on the *Compare* sites — for example, process-of-care measures that reflect unevenly implemented clinical standards of care; adverse outcomes that may, in the aggregate, signal underlying quality or safety problems; resource use measures that may indicate overuse or misuse of costly resources. This perspective also shapes how measures are displayed — highlighting, for example, variations in performance, statistically significant differences from national benchmarks, an emphasis on technical specificity and accuracy in measure labels, descriptions, and displays. The implicit objective is to hold health care providers publicly accountable by drawing attention to differences in performance that professionals recognize to be both clinically important and potentially problematic. Indeed, measures on which performance is uniformly strong ("topped-out" measures) have been retired from public reporting because they no longer discern differences in performance among providers.

Professional Criteria for Selecting Quality Performance Measures

IMPORTANCE

- Capturing an important aspect of quality amenable to provider or health system control.

SCIENTIFIC ACCEPTABILITY

- Having a valid, reliable, and well-defined evidence-based relationship to health care quality.

USABILITY

- Capable of discerning statistically and clinically meaningful differences in performance.

FEASIBILITY

- Measurable using readily available data that are auditable and can be collected without too much burden.

Source: Agency for Healthcare Research and Quality

Consumers' Take on Publicly Reported Measures

Consumers who visit the *Compare* sites have little or no context for understanding the professional perspective on quality measurement and reporting. They are largely unaware of the underlying problems that quality initiatives are intended to address, unless there has been some prior publicity around particular quality issues. They trust their own doctors to make the right decisions about their care, and they assume that Medicare certification, Joint Commission accreditation, or professional credentialing ensures that other health care professionals and institutions meet basic standards of quality and competency. What they expect to find when they come to the *Compare* sites is information about services provided (or covered), staffing, credentialing, areas of specialization or expertise.

Consumers do not know what to make of the quality measures that are reported or understand the rationale for reporting them. They are baffled by process of care measures, because they assume that doctors — not administrative entities like health plans or home health agencies, or even facilities like hospitals or dialysis centers — are responsible for deciding what treatments their patients do or do not need. When they think about the outcomes of care, they prefer to think in terms of sick people being cured or getting better. They know, too, that bad things can happen (like deaths or complications), but they do not understand the rationale for pointing these out on the *Compare* sites or for holding health care providers responsible for things that may be unavoidable.

Consumers are largely unaware of the problems that quality initiatives are intended to address.

Policy makers and professionals may think in terms of quality, efficiency, and value in the health care system writ large, but consumers think first as patients or family caregivers. They do not understand measures that are intended to draw attention to unnecessary or overused technologies, because they assume physicians will use their best judgment to decide what treatments patients need in any given circumstance. When consumers think about the costs of health care, they think in terms of what they are charged or what they have to pay out of pocket. They understand little about how third-party payers (including Medicare) reimburse health care providers, and they often assume that higher payment rates reflect care that is technically more sophisticated or of higher quality.

These assumptions and expectations on the part of visitors to the *Compare* sites who are not familiar with quality professionals' way of thinking pave the way for a great deal of misunderstanding and misinterpretation of publicly reported measures (as we discuss in the next chapter).

How Consumers Think About Quality

How, then, do consumers think about quality in health care? Although there has been some effort to bring them to the quality measurement and reporting table (for example, through the National Quality Forum's institutionalized consumer/purchaser councils), their involvement has almost always come downstream in the process, with an emphasis on initiating them into the professional way of thinking. To date, the only quality measures that have been developed explicitly from a consumer perspective are the Consumer Assessment of Healthcare Providers and Systems family of survey-based patient experience measures — and even these have generated debate among professionals as to whether they should count as quality measures. Indeed, many quality professionals doubt that consumers can judge quality, given their focus on their own personal circumstances and experiences. The common assumption is that what consumers care most about, and pay most attention to, are the interpersonal aspects of care, or what is often referred to as "bedside manner."

When consumers are asked what comes to mind when they think of good or bad quality health care, they do speak of doctors or health care professionals who are caring, friendly, understanding, and "treat you like a person." However, we have found consumers to have a more nuanced understanding of quality than conventional wisdom would imply — an understanding firmly grounded in an awareness of quality in the technical sense, even if it is not in the same sense that professionals see it. What they call attention to, as described below, is a broad array of technical, structural, behavioral, managerial, and systemic factors affecting quality that they can discern firsthand.

Technical Resources and Expertise

Consumers associate good quality with doctors' and staff's qualifications, credentials, training, and experience; their specialized areas of clinical expertise; access to up-to-date diagnostic and therapeutic technologies; preventive care; availability of research-based treatments; and good outcomes. They see inexperience or lack of skills and training as a factor contributing to bad quality, including misdiagnosis, medical errors or malpractice, health care-associated infections, and bad outcomes.

Paying Attention to the Patient

What consumers emphasize most about interpersonal aspects of care is the importance of paying close attention to patients and "taking them seriously." They see this as an important part of clinical quality — paying attention to the unique circumstances and symptoms of individual patients, for example (instead of making a priori assumptions about them); being watchful and vigilant of patients, especially when they are incapacitated; taking the time needed to attend to patients' personal care and treatment. Lack of attention or "rushing through" is also seen as a contributing factor to poor quality, leading to missed diagnoses, errors in judgment, and accidents, and leaving patients and caregivers with a sense of vulnerability.

Consumers have a nuanced understanding of quality, even if not in the same sense that professionals see it.

Management of Health Care Facilities

Consumers recognize that the managerial attributes of health care facilities can contribute to discernible variations in quality — including staffing quality and staffing levels; staff morale and burnout; the quality of supervision, training, and teamwork; operating systems that make things run smoothly; and safety and emergency response procedures.

Communication

Communication is closely linked, in consumers' minds, to clinical quality and personal attention to patients. They value honesty and stress the importance of explaining things clearly and completely to patients and family members, noting that lack of clear communication can lead to serious problems. Equally or even more important to the quality of care, in the minds of many, is the extent to which doctors or other caregivers listen to patients and pay attention to what they have to say. Consumers also emphasize the importance of communication among providers, both in terms of coordinating care and delivering a consistent set of messages to patients. Many consumers are also beginning to notice that information technology (including electronic health records and email communication with providers) is improving communication.

Physical Attributes of a Health Care Facility

Consumers often mention the physical or structural characteristics of health care facilities when talking about quality. The attribute they mention most often is cleanliness, noting that unsanitary conditions can lead to infections. Other characteristics associated with good quality include affiliation with an academic research institution, the availability of up-to-date technological innovations, and the newness of the facility. Family members, in particular, may also take notice of conveniences and amenities, such as a hospital's food or internet service.

Health System Issues

Consumers also raise issues related to the broader workings of the health care system. They often notice, for example, the lack of collaboration among specialists or providers who work in different health care settings, the efficiency (or, more often, the perceived inefficiency) of the referral and prior-approval process in some health plans, and inequities in how well the system works for different groups of people.

Operational Efficiency

Consumers value efficiency, in the sense of not "wasting my time," and discussions about quality prompt frequent mention of wait times and timely access to care. Consumers appreciate offices or clinics that run smoothly and get patients in and out quickly, electronic access to providers for referrals or prescriptions, 24- hour nurse call-in lines, and "fast service." At the same time, they are concerned that providers may sacrifice thoroughness, for the sake of convenience, speed, and efficiency. They do not want to be "rushed through" if it means not getting the attention they need.

Costs

The topic of cost can also arise in discussions about health care quality. Consumers often refer to their out-of-pocket costs, in terms of co-pays and deductibles, and sometimes note high line-item charges on hospital bills. A recurring concern is that what happens in health care is "all about money." In this context, high- quality providers are seen as those who look out for patients' interests and provide options, instead of looking only to their own financial gain.

Institute of Medicine's Six Aims

Safe Care
Effective Care
Patient-Centered Care
Timely Care
Efficient Care
Equitable Care

Defining a Common Framework for Communicating About Quality

In policy circles, dialogue around quality and efficiency in health care has begun to coalesce around two related sets of strategic objectives reflecting some degree of professional consensus about systemic problems and areas in need of improvement: (1) the Institute of Medicine's (IOM's) six aims for improvement,[6] and (2) the six quality domains defined as part of the National Quality Strategy.[7] Other researchers' findings have suggested that at least some of these concepts, when explained in consumer-friendly language, help enhance consumers' ability to conceptualize quality problems or interpret comparative displays of performance on selected measures.[8] Our research has also explored the potential usefulness of the IOM and National Quality Strategy domains as both a conceptual framework for engaging consumers in questions about quality, efficiency, and value in health care and an organizational framework for publicly reporting expanded measures of quality, efficiency, and value on the *Compare* sites.

As noted, we have found consumers' subjective perceptions of quality to be based on concrete phenomena they can observe or experience firsthand, rather than on abstract value propositions such as those embodied in the IOM and National Quality Strategy domains. Nevertheless, they quite readily connect their firsthand perceptions and experiences to the underlying technical/structural, behavioral, managerial, and systemic factors that lead to quality within these domains. They understand, for example, that *effective* care, as the IOM defines it, is a function of the quality components they identify — including technical skills and experience of the professional staff, staff attentiveness to individual patients, the quality of the operating systems and procedures, communication among professionals and between clinicians and patients, and the availability of up-to-date technologies and research-based treatments. Although consumers may be less likely to buy into the concept of *efficiency* in the sense of "avoiding waste," for fear that it implies restricting access to needed or desirable services, we also found them to be quite sensitive to issues related to managerial efficiency and excessive health care costs, both of which may provide an entrée into broader conversations about efficiency and value in health care. Consumers are also aware of systemic issues that may contribute to variations in quality and inequities in health care.

This suggests the possibility of developing a common language for communicating about quality, using the IOM or National Quality Strategy domains as a framework. Relating the content of the *Compare* sites to these quality domains can help make them a vehicle for engaging consumers in discussions that move beyond the personal decisions they might face at a particular moment, but that draw on their experience to think about health care quality in broader terms.

Consumers' perceptions of quality are based on concrete phenomena they can observe firsthand.

National Quality Strategy Priorities

Safety, or Reduction of Harm
Engaging Patients and Families
Care Coordination
Effective Prevention and Treatment
Promoting Population and Community Health and Reducing Disparities
Promoting Affordability, Efficiency, and Cost Reduction

IV. CONVEYING PERFORMANCE INFORMATION

The immediate focus of most of our research over these past 10 years has been on very practical questions about how to convey specific information reported on the *Compare* sites to a target audience that includes lay consumers and the information intermediaries (including health care professionals) who influence their decisions. The goal is to convey the information in a way that consumers can understand it, interpret it accurately, and (hopefully) apply or use it. The challenge is to bridge the gap between the needs, expectations, understanding, and real-life decisions that consumers bring to the table and the perspectives that have shaped the way that quality professionals think about, measure, and report health care quality and efficiency.

Much attention has been given in the recent professional literature to widespread problems with health literacy and numeracy (or mathematical literacy) as barriers to consumers' ability to process and use basic health information to make appropriate health care decisions. Our research suggests, however, that the gap between professionals' and the lay public's understanding of health care quality, cost, and efficiency is not simply explained by differences in education or language and math skills (as real as those differences may be). There are basic differences in the ways that quality professionals and consumers think about and approach these issues that create barriers even for more-educated audiences. The kind of information presented on the *Compare* sites can be difficult to interpret at any education level, regardless of attempts to use plain language or render the metrics and displays more user friendly.

Educators working in the area of adult learning and literacy note that adult numeracy is related as much to the context for using quantitative information — that is, the purpose and nature of the task at hand — as to the specific mathematical knowledge or cognitive and affective problem-solving processes that may be required. The dilemma in presenting health care performance information to consumers is that the context for quality professionals and for consumers is not the same. Conveying the information in a way that consumers can understand, interpret, and use requires (1) establishing a common ground for understanding the problem or issues to be addressed, (2) making the connection between the reported metrics and the problem, and (3) presenting the data in a format that consumers can interpret accurately and apply to the problem or issue at hand.

In this chapter, we review what we have learned about the particular challenges related to language, metrics, and displays for presenting information on quality, cost, and efficiency to consumers, focusing on the *Compare* websites.

> The gap between professionals' and the lay public's understanding of publicly reported measures is not explained by differences in education or language and math skills.

Conveying Performance Information

> *ESTABLISHING THE CONTEXT*
>
> - What underlying health care problem or issue is being addressed?
> - How do reported measures bear on this problem or issue?

EXPLAINING THE METRICS
- What is being measured?
- What do the numbers represent?

PRACTICAL IMPLICATIONS
- What does this tell me about differences among plans or providers in my community?
- What does this tell me about the magnitude or importance of this problem (overall, or in my community)?
- What does this mean to me?

Establishing the Context: What Is This and Why Is It Important?

Historically, the *Compare* sites have conveyed few conceptual clues to help orient lay users to the sites' overall purpose and content. Also, they have not been designed to help consumers tailor information to their particular needs or interests. Most of the *Compare* sites begin with a search function that allows users to generate a list of plans or providers available within a geographic area, from which they can select a few to compare.

Terms that make sense to quality professionals may convey something very different to consumers.

But our research consistently confirms that the uninitiated user who lacks any prior knowledge of the website's purpose or content has no way of anticipating what kind of information this search will yield.

Most experienced website users do not read introductory text very closely. Instead, they navigate as quickly as possible to what they assume to be the core content, taking their cues from the organizational features and labels they see. Categories and terms that make sense to Medicare program personnel or quality professionals may convey something very different to consumers. Consumers often assume, for example, that a *patient experience* label will lead to personal testimonials (like those they are familiar with from websites like Angie's List); that information on *Medicare payment* will explain what Medicare does (and does not) pay for; that terms like *processes of care* or even *quality measures* refer to administrative procedures.

More recently, CMS has sought consumer input to develop more-intuitive labels and organizational cues to convey information about content more accurately. The tab structure and several of the newer labels on the *Hospital Compare* site, for example, are now suggestive of the quality concepts reflected in the National Quality Strategy domains, and labels like *survey of patients' experience*, *timely & effective care*, and *complications & deaths* have tested well in terms of their clarity. Most consumers also readily understand what *health inspections* and *staffing* refer to (on the *Nursing Home Compare* site). However, other terms and labels on the results pages of *Hospital Compare* and other *Compare* sites — notably, *readmissions*, *use of medical imaging*, *Medicare payment*, and *number of Medicare patients* — remain obscure and subject to misinterpretation.

Establishing the context — giving website users a general idea about what is being reported and why it is important — is critical to their understanding of the *Compare* tools, as they are currently designed. When we direct research participants' attention to narrative explanations in testing situations, they typically find this very helpful in making sense of what can otherwise seem a bewildering display of technical information. However, they rarely find or see this information on their own.

Organizing and Layering Information

Another major challenge consumers face in comprehending or making use of the health care performance measures on the *Compare* websites lies in the sheer volume and complexity of the information that is (and, increasingly, will be) publicly reported. In our approach to consumer research, we typically try to show research participants actual performance metrics as they would likely be presented alongside other information on the *Compare* sites, in order to get a realistic sense of how they would react to it in practice. Consumers will scan data displays, we have found, to get a sense of what is being reported, but they will do little more than gloss over them if confronted with a lot of detail at once. Often, in testing situations, they will focus on the first two or three measures displayed but will not seem to notice or pay attention to any others.

Recognizing this problem, consumer advocates have recommended simplifying quality reports aimed at consumers through summary ratings or composite measures of performance. We, too, have found that consumers often want and expect to see such ratings, and may even wrongly assume that the first displays they see *are* overall performance ratings. (In the very first display on the *Home Health Compare* results page, for example, consumers sometimes misinterpret the symbols indicating services that are (✔) and are not (⊘) offered as overall ratings of acceptable and unacceptable performance in these areas, and look no further.) At this writing, only the *Nursing Home Compare* and *Plan Finder* websites provide summary ratings, but there has been considerable interest within CMS in developing and reporting them on the other sites, as well.

Consumers will gloss over data displays if confronted with a lot of detail at once.

However, we have also found that consumers often get the wrong idea about what summary ratings actually mean, in the absence of any prior knowledge of what goes into quality measurement and reporting. They tend to interpret such measures in light of what they expect to see, which can be misleading. Consumers typically assume, for example, that overall ratings of health care providers or facilities reflect medical experts' judgments about the comprehensiveness of the services offered, the credentials and experience of medical professionals, and a host of other characteristics that are not usually captured by the metrics.

Although consumers often expect and want to see summary measures of performance, many are also interested in drilling down to the more detailed information on the *Compare* sites. Some will ask, specifically, what a composite score or summary rating is based on. Others will note that overall ratings can obscure important variations among departments, services, or clinicians within a health care facility. Many consumers look for ways to select or tailor information to their specific interests or needs. However, the data currently available on the *Compare* sites often do not readily fit the search categories or provide the type of information that consumers care about. Others look for search or filtering mechanisms that would allow them to sort information by medical conditions or procedures not currently included in performance metrics.

Explaining What Is Being Measured and How It Relates to Quality

Orienting consumers to the value of publicly reported information on health care quality also requires clarifying, at the measure level, what is being measured and how it relates to quality of care. Consumers take their first cues from the category and measure labels themselves, which vary considerably from one *Compare* site to another. Confronted with displays of technical information they do not understand, website users will typically look for (and click on) any link that looks as if it will provide an explanation — for example, the measure label itself, an information icon, or a link to "more information." If they do not find what they are looking for with one or two clicks, they typically become frustrated and look no further.

Findings from consumer testing of technical measures on the *Compare* sites raise questions about how best to balance clarity with brevity, and specificity with "skimmability." Although many of the measure labels on *Hospital Compare*, for example, have been drafted to convey as precisely as possible what is being measured, this can result in wordy labels that are hard for users to skim through. Labels on the *Plan Finder* site, by contrast, tend to be short and easy to skim, but users often misinterpret them. For example, the "Breast Cancer Screening" measure, which actually reports the percentage of women who received a mammogram, is usually understood to mean how good the plan's coverage is for breast cancer screening.

Technical language and professional jargon can also hinder consumers' understanding of publicly reported measures. Terms that may have specific meaning to health researchers, clinicians, quality professionals, or Medicare staff often have a different meaning in the everyday language of consumers.

> Terms that have a specific meaning to health researchers often have a different meaning in the everyday language of consumers.
>
> Consumers react emotionally to some terms, even though their meaning is quite clear.

For example, in consumer testing of hospital readmissions measures, a number of research participants assumed that the term *rate* (as in "hospital readmission rate") referred to the amount charged or paid for a hospital readmission, until the term was more clearly qualified ("rate of hospital readmission"). Consumers may also be unfamiliar with the use of the term *measures* to mean performance metrics, and think that *quality measures* (like *safety measures*) refer to specific administrative actions taken by health care providers. Other commonly used, but confusing, terms include *beneficiary*, when applied to a person on Medicare (confused with the beneficiary of a will or life insurance policy); *Original Medicare* (interpreted as applying to the very first Medicare legislation or people covered by it); health care *practitioners* (not understood as referring to health care professionals); and health care *providers* (confused with nonprofessional personal care providers).

Technical terms and acronyms that refer to specific medical conditions, tests, or procedures — such as urea reduction rate (URR) or Kt/V on the *Dialysis Compare* site, or venous thromboembolism (VTE) or *Clostridium difficile* on *Hospital Compare* — will also usually require some explanation. However, some acronyms (like MRSA, for methicillin-resistant *Staphylococcus aureus*) are much more familiar to consumers from news stories.

Although one of the primary aims of consumer testing is to ensure that language is clear and understandable, consumers may also react emotionally to some terms, even though their meaning is quite clear. Consumers understand "complications" and "deaths," for example, but sometimes say they would avoid looking at this information, because it is too frightening. Death rates on the *Dialysis Facility Compare* site are reported instead as "survival rates," but this term, too, appears to conjure up unwelcome thoughts to many consumers.

Plain language alone, however, is not sufficient to make the meaning of quality measures clear to lay users. Translating the technical terms from measure specifications into plain English yields descriptions that may be technically accurate, but still not very understandable to the average consumer. Consider, for example, the "elective delivery" measure recently introduced to the *Hospital Compare* website (see below). From a quality perspective, the underlying rationale for publicly reporting this measure is that it addresses a common reason for hospital admission (childbirth) among the younger and healthier population and a common practice that deserves attention because it may put newborns at unnecessary risk. This, however, is not something that most lay persons are aware of. The typical approach to drafting consumer-oriented content is to start with the technical definition, substituting medical terms that may be less familiar to lay users (such as "elective" or "gestation") with more consumer-friendly language (such as "not medically necessary" or "pregnancy"). But this, by itself, does not explain what is being measured, why, or what this has to do with quality of care.

Consumer testing revealed that several issues needed to be clarified for consumers to make sense of this measure: (1) that the measure refers to deliveries that are too early (pre-term, but not premature), induced (not spontaneous), and elective (not medically necessary); (2) that it refers to an ill-advised practice, not a benign discretionary decision on the part of patients and their doctors; and (3) that what is being measured and reported is the percentage of early deliveries that were not medically necessary (and not for example, the percentage of *all* deliveries that fell into one or both categories). These findings shaped the rather lengthy measure label and explanatory language that were subsequently reported on the *Hospital Compare* website, as shown below.

Although some publicly reported measures are more intuitive than others, the technical nature of many of them poses challenges similar to the "elective delivery" example cited above: for example, the anemia management or dialysis adequacy measures on the *Dialysis Facility Compare* site, the use of antipsychotic medications for long-term nursing home residents, or the many different blood clot prevention and treatment measures on *Hospital Compare.*

CMS has developed detailed plain-language explanations for many, if not most, of the reported measures on the *Compare* sites. When we direct research participants' attention to them in testing situations, they often remark that they should be readily accessible to users at the outset —*"Why didn't they say this in the first place?"* But the most immediate and visible links adjacent to the data displays do not necessarily take users to these explanations.

Plain language alone is not sufficient to make the meaning of quality measures clear to lay users.

THE CHALLENGE OF CONVEYING QUALITY INFORMATION TO CONSUMERS: "ELECTIVE DELIVERY"

TECHNICAL SPECIFICATIONS

Measure Title

- Elective Delivery

Brief Description

- This measure assesses patients with elective vaginal deliveries or elective cesarean sections at ≥ 37 and < 39 weeks of gestation completed

Numerator

- Patients with elective deliveries for one or more of the following:
  - Medical induction of labor
  - Cesarean section while not in active labor or experiencing spontaneous rupture of membranes

Denominator

- Patients delivering newborns with ≥ 37 and < 39 weeks of gestation completed

LANGUAGE ON HOSPITAL COMPARE

Measure Label

- Percent of newborns whose deliveries were scheduled too early (1–3 weeks early), when a scheduled delivery was not medically necessary

What is this and why is it important?

- Guidelines developed by doctors and researchers say it's best to wait until the 39th completed week of pregnancy to deliver your baby because important fetal development takes place in your baby's brain and lungs during the last few weeks of pregnancy.
- Sometimes women go into early labor on their own, and early deliveries can't be prevented. Sometimes, doctors decide that inducing labor or delivering a baby early by C-section (called "elective delivery") is in the best interest of the mother and the baby. In these cases, early deliveries are medically necessary.
- However, doctors may also decide to induce labor or deliver babies by C-section early as a convenience to themselves or their patient. **This practice is not recommended.** Hospitals should work with doctors and patients to avoid early elective deliveries when they are not medically necessary.
- This measure shows the percent of pregnancy women who had elective deliveries 1–3 weeks early (either vaginally or by C-section) whose early deliveries were not medically necessary. Higher numbers may indicate that hospitals aren't doing enough to discourage this unsafe practice.

Lower percentages are better.

Understanding the Metrics

Consumers' interest in and ability to use the publicly reported information on the *Compare* sites will also depend on their understanding what the metrics are telling them; this, in turn, will depend on what questions they want to address. Although the emphasis among consumer advocates has been on using public reports to inform choice, "Which provider is best?" may not always be the most salient question to consumers, given their circumstances. The questions they ask about the data in testing situations suggest they also wonder, "How big a problem is this?" "How much of a risk does this pose?" "How much of a difference is there among providers?"

> ' Which provider is best?' may not be the most salient question. Consumers also wonder, 'How big a problem is this?' 'How much of a risk does this pose?'

How the metrics are reported can facilitate or impede consumers' understanding and use of the information to answer such questions. Quality and resource use metrics are reported on the *Compare* sites in many different ways, shaped in part by the quality professionals who are the measure stewards and other professional stakeholders. Metrics may be positively or negatively framed, with higher numbers indicating better or worse performance. They may be reported as percentages, natural frequencies, measures of time, incidence, ratios, or comparisons to a benchmark. Here, we review what we have learned about consumers' ability to interpret and use quantitative information presented in different formats.

Percentages

Many of the process-of-care and outcomes measures on the *Compare* sites are displayed as percentages, indicating the rate of compliance with a standard of care or recommended treatment (that is, the percentage of eligible patients who received the indicated service) or a risk-standardized outcomes estimate. Consumers are mostly familiar with percentages and are able to interpret them reasonably accurately, especially when they are displayed as whole numbers between 1 and 100. However, percentages less than 1 presented in decimal format may be harder to interpret.

Although percentages facilitate comparisons among providers or facilities, some consumers also want to see the actual number of cases or patients that they are based on, noting that real numbers give them a better sense of what lies behind the percentages and how many patients the metric applies to in a particular case.

Rates per Thousand (Natural Frequency)

Quality measures reflecting rarer events (such as complication rates) are often presented as rates per thousand, rather than percentages. However, consumers are less familiar with this format, and often assume the numbers reported reflect either the actual number of cases or a percentage. As a result, although they may be able to interpret the numbers for purposes of comparison, they often conclude that the actual frequency is much higher than it is. Moreover, both consumers and health care professionals (including physicians) are often perplexed to see rates per thousand that have been calculated based on fewer than 1,000 eligible cases, and may assume that these numbers are wrong.

Consumers have particular difficulty interpreting frequencies less than 1 in 1,000, expressed as decimals, as is the case for some health care—associated infections (HAIs) and hospital-acquired conditions (HACs) and other rare events. When looking at draft displays of HACs, for example, many research participants assumed that the decimals represented percentages (for example, assuming a frequency of 0.050/thousand = 5 percent, or even 50 percent), and many were unable to say how often such events would occur based on the rates shown. On the *Hospital Compare* website, rates for HACs and HAIs (rare occurrences) often differ only slightly between hospitals. Consumers may understand that these are rare, but they often still overestimate both the risk and the differences between the hospitals, assuming one hospital's performance is markedly better or worse than another's based on the numbers shown, when in reality there is very little difference between them.

Our research has also shown that presenting rare events as normalized rates, or variable frequencies normalized to 1 (for example, 1 out of 12,000 cases versus 0.084 per 1,000 cases) was a somewhat more familiar format to consumers (similar to gambling odds, for example) that better conveyed a sense of how often events occur. However, presenting the data based on normalized rates makes it harder for respondents to compare health care providers or facilities to each other or to benchmarks, because the denominators vary. Showing the incidence or the actual numbers of patients affected, in addition to rates, also aids comprehension of this type of information.

Showing the actual numbers of patients affected aids comprehension.

Numerators and Denominators

The numerators and denominators used to calculate rates, whether percentages or frequencies, are a source of confusion for many consumers, which can impede their ability to understand or interpret the data accurately.

Consumers often want to know how many patients are included in a particular measure, in part because it conveys a sense of how many patients are affected by that quality indicator and in part because it tells them how many such patients a particular provider has seen. Some displays on the *Compare* sites show both the performance rate and the denominator in more detailed tabular data displays (for example, 99% of 880 patients or 99% of 385 patients). However, seeing the data displayed this way, with different denominators, confused some consumers, and led others to think they would have to calculate the statistics themselves. Consumers were better able to interpret these numbers when the denominator information was presented in text next to graphic displays (for example, inserting the words "based on 880 Medicare patients" next to a bar showing the performance rate as a percentage), rather than in data tables. In this latter case, consumers liked seeing the denominator numbers, both as an aid to interpreting the performance rates and as a proxy measure for provider experience.

Consumers also frequently misunderstand which patient populations are included in the numerator and denominator of different quality measures displayed on the *Compare* websites. Some measures include all patients, whereas others (often displayed in the same measure set) include only a subset of patients with a specific condition or receiving a certain type of surgery or treatment. For example, for the *Elective delivery* measure cited previously, only patients who had early deliveries are included in the denominator. Consumers often overlook this information, however, and assume that the rate shown is a percentage of all women who gave birth. This oversight can make it especially hard to interpret safety measures reflecting rare complications or adverse events and to determine which pose the greater risk, in terms of actual numbers of patients affected.

Resource use is typically compared to a standard, or benchmark, that represents an acceptable, or "expected," rate of performance. This serves as a basis for flagging high and low performers. How the benchmark is defined (and how high the bar is set) will depend on the statistical characteristics of the measure and how it will be used. But for purposes of public reporting, the benchmark usually represents an adjusted national performance rate.

Consumers, too, like to see a benchmark to serve as a point of reference for making comparisons. They vary, however, in what type of benchmark they would like to see. Many consumers who approach the *Compare* sites wondering "what is best for me" are looking to make comparisons in the metropolitan area where they live, and have little interest in benchmarks representing national or state averages. Some also have little interest in "average" performance of any sort, and would rather see best or ideal performance as the benchmark.

Because of the potential for confusion or misinterpretation of some performance measures (especially dire outcomes measures, such as deaths and complications), some metrics on the *Compare* sites are reported in terms that convey comparisons to benchmarks rather than actual performance rates. A commonly used format is the so-called "bucket" display, which categorizes performance based on statistically significant differences from benchmarks (worse, no different, better; or lower, no different, higher). Consumers generally understand what these displays are conveying, and they can be useful for summarizing performance across many different measures in a single facility profile. However, categorizing performance based on comparisons to a benchmark may be of little use to consumers for comparative purposes.

Most consumers want more detail than either bucket displays or observed-to-expected ratios provide.

Bucket Displays, and Ratios

Among quality professionals, the performance of an individual health care provider or facility on a specific measure of quality or One issue has to do with how buckets are defined. Website users invariably assume that the middle category reflects "average" performance. Because the categories are based on statistical significance, however, the middle bucket actually captures both average providers and (more often) those whose numbers are too small to determine whether their performance is statistically significantly different. Their performance rates may be high or low, but the difference from the benchmark is uncertain. The "no different" label is intended to capture this ambiguity, but it is a distinction that most consumers (and other audiences) miss. The only providers or facilities that would be flagged as high or low are those whose volume is high enough to generate numbers that are statistically significant.

More important, simple comparisons to a benchmark can mislead consumers as to how facilities compare to each other. The fact that a facility is flagged as high or low in a bucket display does not mean that its performance is significantly different from that of the facilities that fall into the middle bucket. More often, they are not.

Another metric used to convey performance in comparison to benchmarks are ratios of observed-to-expected performance, such as the standardized infection ratios used to report HAIs, or the *Spending per hospital patient with Medicare* measure, both on *Hospital Compare*. These are usually reported as decimals, where 1.0 represents expected performance, numbers less than 1.0 represent lower-than-expected performance, and numbers greater than 1.0 reflect higher-than-expected performance. Consumers are not accustomed to seeing ratios presented this way and are likely to misinterpret the metrics as percentages (or, in the case of the spending measure, as dollars), unless the ratios are explained to them. Once the ratios are explained, consumers generally understand that, like the bucket displays, these ratios show comparisons to benchmarks, rather than actual performance rates. Unlike bucket displays, however, ratios better convey the magnitude of the difference and the degree of variation among providers or facilities.

Most consumers want more detail than either the bucket displays or the observed-to-expected ratios provide. They typically want to know what actual performance rates are, how many cases or people are affected (in the case of HAIs), how much difference there actually is among providers. In some cases, bucket displays are presented on the *Compare* sites as first-level summaries, and consumers can drill down to more detail showing actual performance rates. When that information is available, some of the limitations of the comparisons to benchmarks become more apparent to them.

Directionality and Negative Measures

Another challenge in presenting quality information to consumers in a way they can interpret accurately has to do with the intended directionality of the measure — whether higher rates reflect better or worse performance. Consumers understand directionality when looking at a single measure whose intended meaning is reasonably clear. In some cases, however, the intention is not clear: Are higher rates of follow-up mammograms a good or a bad thing? Do higher rates of spending indicate waste or higher quality care?

The intended directionality of a measure may not be clear: Are higher rates of follow-up mammograms a good or a bad thing? Do higher rates of spending indicate waste or higher quality care?

Consumers generally equate higher performance rates with better performance and may misinterpret data, especially when scanning displays of multiple measures. For example, when testing comprehension of nursing home quality measures, some respondents reasoned that the negative quality measures referred to strengths and capabilities of the nursing homes, rather than to preventable adverse outcomes. If the nursing home had a high percentage of residents with pressure sores, they interpreted this to mean the home must be particularly good at dealing with pressure sores, thus attracting a higher proportion of residents with this condition. Users become especially confused when looking at data displays that mix positive and negative measures. Under these circumstances, they may begin to question the intended meaning of measures that they previously understood.

Consumers equate higher performance rates with better performance.

Limitations of the Data and Statistical Concepts

Most consumers (and clinicians) lack a detailed knowledge of statistics and are unfamiliar with methods used for quantifying quality and performance data. For the most part, they do not have an interest in this information, and those who do can usually access descriptions of methodology through links on the *Compare* website. Nevertheless, many consumers and clinicians raise questions about the data that may affect their response to the information.

Two questions that can affect users' initial response to the *Compare* tools and their perceived usefulness have to do with where the data come from and to whom they apply. Because the tools are hosted on the Medicare website, most consumers assume that the information applies only to Medicare beneficiaries. Consumers are more inclined to trust data that have been gathered independently, but they often assume that the information is self-reported by health care providers, or is even promotional (much like information on proprietary provider websites). If patient survey data are displayed the most prominently or viewed first, users may also assume that all of the measures are based on patient surveys. In practice, the sources of information and sample populations vary across measure sets and *Compare* sites, but this information is usually provided in the more technical data details for professionals and is not readily accessible on the consumer-facing pages.

[Saying that] data have been adjusted to account for differences in risk can convey the impression that statistics have been fiddled with to make them look better.

Consumers often have an intuitive sense of some statistical concepts and potential limitations of the data, even if they are not statistically savvy. For example, most understand that a health care provider's or facility's performance on outcomes measures (deaths, complications, hospital admissions, or readmissions) will look worse if that provider treats sicker or needier patients — and they will often bring this up on their own, for example when looking at data for well-known "safety net" hospitals in their own area. Many consumers also understand that observations based on a small sample of patients will yield murky estimates (which partly accounts for their interest in knowing how many patients a measure applies to). Most consumers also recognize that small differences in reported performance rates, even if they are statistically significant, may not reflect meaningful differences in performance (which partly accounts for their interest in seeing actual performance rates, and not simply comparisons to benchmarks).

Consumers assume that missing data reflect badly on a health care facility or a provider.

However, consumers usually do not understand statistical terms like *risk adjustment*, *interval estimates*, and *statistical significance*. Nor do they, along with many clinicians, understand (or necessarily believe) the methods of adjusting for these limitations. However, efforts to explain these concepts can raise more questions than they answer — in part, because words like *risk*, *expected*, *confidence*, and *significance* have very different meanings to the lay public than they do to quality professionals or statisticians. Explanations that the data have been *adjusted* to account for differences in risk or small sample sizes, although intended to enhance trust in the fairness of the reported measures, can convey the impression that statistics have been fiddled with just to make them look better.

Consumers are also skeptical of missing data, regardless of the terms used to explain their absence (*not available*, *no data are available for this measure*, *too few cases*, *data was suppressed for one or more quarters by CMS*, and so on). Consumers consistently assume that missing data reflect negatively on the facility or provider — that the facility does not keep adequate records, is trying to hide poor scores, that "too few cases" means patients are avoiding that particular provider, or that the provider does not have adequate experience. Missing data is one of the first things consumers notice in a data display, and they will often volunteer, on their own, that they would "stay away" from those providers or facilities.

Displays: What Do Numbers Mean?

In addition to the metrics themselves, how the data are displayed can influence consumers' interpretation and understanding of the publicly reported information. The *Compare* sites use several different formats.

At this writing, comparative performance metrics for selected providers are typically presented first in numeric tables, and users have the option (through links on the results page) to view more detailed data tables or to see graphic displays of the data (bar graphs). Both of these types of displays present the measure-level metrics for selected providers, alongside state and national benchmarks (where available), and may include directional cues (especially for negative measures), but they provide no additional interpretive cues.

In addition, on some *Compare* sites and for some measures, the information may be provided in an interpretive or evaluative display format, where, in lieu of performance rates or other metrics, words or symbols convey information about how well a facility or provider performed. These formats may be used alone or in combination to convey summary or composite information as well as measure-level performance data.

Here, we review what we have learned about the advantages and disadvantages of each type of display format.

Numeric Tables

To many consumers, the sight of a table full of numbers will seem daunting — too much work to make sense of. However, some consumers prefer to see all comparative data displayed this way — notably, those who are most interested in the details. One advantage to tabular displays is that they allow users to compare the performance of many different plans, providers, or facilities across many different measures at one time. If the numbers are comparable in format and all go in the same direction, the information can be easy to scan. Tables can easily become too busy and hard to read, however, when that is not the case or when many different data elements are reported.

Graphic Displays

Many consumers prefer visual displays of data in graphical format, and most (but not all) are familiar with simple bar graphs similar to those used on the *Compare* sites. When considering a single quality measure, bar graphs facilitate at-a-glance comparisons among facilities or to benchmark. However, the use of bar graphs also presents several challenges.

We have found that consumers tend to focus more on the blue bars that represent selected providers and often either fail to notice the yellow bars that represent state or national benchmarks or not understand what they refer to. In testing alternative versions of nursing home displays, respondents were more likely to pay attention to and use benchmarks for purposes of comparison when the benchmark rate was shown as a solid line intersecting the bars.

Unlike tables, bar graphs do not allow users to scan performance rates across many different measures and many different providers at one time. The *Compare* sites generate a separate graph for each measure, with comparative bars representing up to three selected providers (in blue) and state and national benchmarks (in yellow). To view several measures, users have to scroll through several different graphs. In testing situations, they often focus only on the first graph displayed (sometimes assuming it represents an overall summary of performance) and may not notice that others are available.

Using different scales for different measures makes comparisons misleading.

Issues of scale can also make it challenging to display some information graphically. The rule of thumb is to use the same scale for all measures, preferably showing the full range of potential values (for example, a scale of 0 to 100 percent). This can be difficult when performance is measured differently for different measures or when performance rates vary markedly across measures. However, using different scales for different measures can exaggerate differences and make comparisons among measures misleading. When viewing draft displays for *Air Embolism* during consumer testing of HACs, for example, respondents at first preferred the graphs (figure 1) to the data tables because they thought they were easy to understand. When their attention was directed to the rates of occurrence, however, most respondents thought the graphs distorted the magnitude of the data.

Displaying ranges of performance in addition to point estimates can also be difficult for consumers to interpret graphically. For example, in reporting 30-day mortality measures on the *Hospital Compare* site, mortality rates are reported (and shown graphically) as point estimates along with the interval estimates. Consumer testing for the development of the first display of this measure yielded the display shown in figure 2, with the point estimate inside a bar representing the interval estimate. About half of the testing participants (including physicians) recognized that the bar represented some sort of range, although few fully understood it, and most focused on the point estimate. In redesigning the *Hospital Compare* site, the website developers changed the design to make it more visually appealing (as shown in figure 3), but without retesting to determine its impact on users' interpretation.

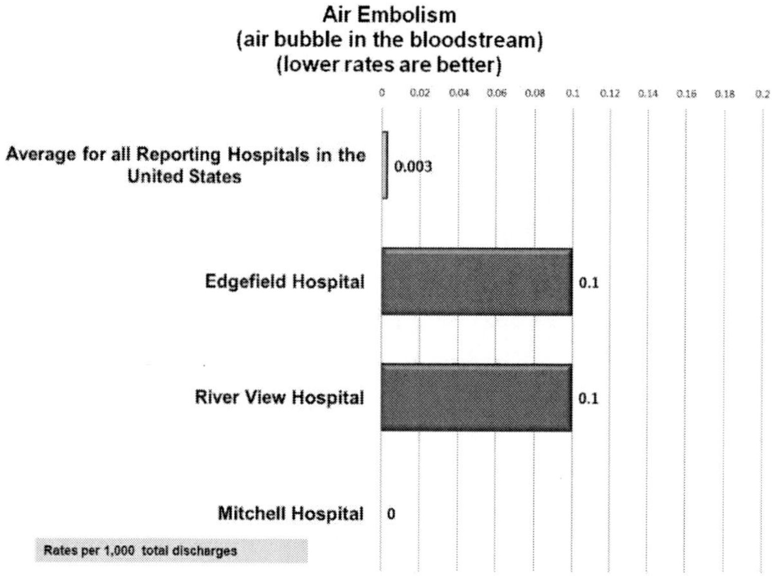

Figure 1.

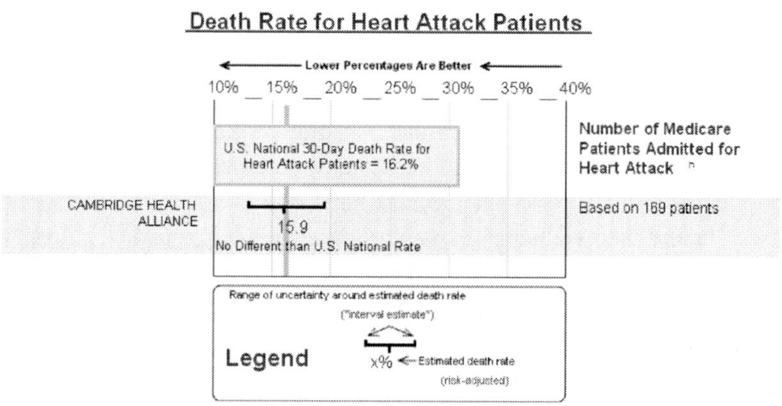

Figure 2.

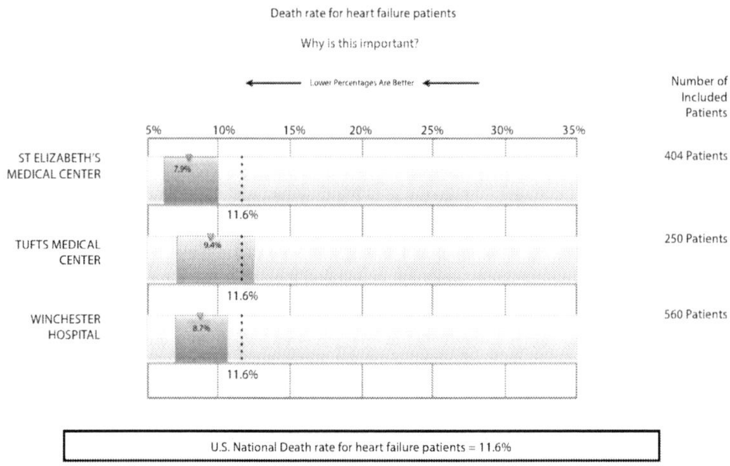

Figure 3.

Most consumers are familiar with star ratings from their use in other settings. The principal advantage of star ratings is that they allow users to skim information across many different categories or measures and across many different providers at once, and to see at a glance stronger and weaker areas of performance without having to interpret the numbers. Using star ratings also eliminates the burden of aggregating and interpreting data that may vary from measure to measure, including changes in directionality and units of measurement (percentages, seconds, number of complaints, staffing numbers). In testing situations, consumers may look at star ratings in particular categories, or count up the total number of stars to determine which provider is doing best.

However, the use of star ratings also has drawbacks. They can enhance the impression that ratings are based on expert judgment, as star ratings are commonly used in other settings (such as hotel ratings and movie or restaurant reviews), unless their statistical basis is made clear. The statistical cutoffs that determine the number of stars displayed may also mislead users about the differences between providers. Also, they do not convey information about the magnitude of differences or the degree of variation.

The use of stars can enhance the impression that ratings are based on expert judgment.

Star displays may also be subject to misinterpretation when used to indicate performance on negative measures. One example of this occurred during consumer testing of star displays for a quality measure to be reported on *Physician Compare* that reflects poor blood sugar control in patients with diabetes. In this case, many consumers were confused as to whether more stars indicated better performance or higher percentages on this measure (and therefore worse performance). Star ratings also led to more errors in interpreting negative nursing home measures, when compared to the use of words ("better," "worse") to indicate performance. However, we have also found that this issue can be mitigated by adding an explanation to help users interpret the directionality of the measure (for example, "More stars are better because that means fewer complaints").

Symbols other than stars, although not used on CMS's *Compare* tools, are often used on other public reporting websites to indicate relative performance. Like star displays, symbols can be easier to skim than numeric displays, giving users a sense of overall performance across many different categories. However, we have found that the usability of such displays depends on whether the symbols themselves are intuitive. Even commonly used symbols, like the circles used in *Consumer Reports* product reviews, may mean different things in different settings (an empty circle may indicate no points awarded, or no problems reported). When symbols are not intuitive, these displays place a high cognitive burden on users, who have to locate a legend to determine what the symbols mean and remember that information as they view the data.

Translation and Cultural Relevance

We have also conducted research with Spanish-speaking consumers, an audience that introduces unique considerations to the communication of information around quality and choice. In addition to the issues raised above — establishing context and explaining what is being measured and why — the additional challenges Spanish-speaking consumers face in synthesizing and using this information must be considered. For Spanish versions of the *Compare* tools, the information should go beyond mere translation, taking cultural appropriateness, norms, and relevance into consideration.

Translation alone is not sufficient to make the meaning of information clear to all users. Other factors, such as users' cultural patterns and beliefs or lack of familiarity or experience with the U.S. health system, can hinder comprehension of certain terms or concepts used on the *Compare* tools. For example, several Spanish-speaking participants were unfamiliar with certain concepts:

- Unfamiliarity with appeals or the appeals process led to difficulty comprehending measures related to appeals time lines and appeals upheld on the Plan Finder tool.
- Explanatory information suggesting patients should talk to a provider or ask questions about health care topics goes against cultural norms that regard doctors as experts and "authorities" who should not be questioned or challenged

Some terms are better understood in English than in Spanish.

- The notion of "strangers coming into their home" to provide home health services raised concern for some Spanish-speaking participants, because it goes against the cultural tradition of the family providing care, until they were assured that these services would be provided with the recommendation of their doctor.
- Other issues include misinterpreting phrases or terms related to quality of care, such as equating "communicate well" with providers being able to speak Spanish or "quality ratings" ("calificaciones del plan," in Spanish) as denoting eligibility, or "qualifying" for a plan.

In addition, for younger or bilingual consumers, some terms are better understood, or more commonly used, in English than Spanish. For example, adult children or caregivers who are bilingual may prefer to use English language versions of written material or websites when reviewing information for their own use but may choose to view Spanish language versions of those same materials when assisting monolingual parents. In addition, several technical terms or acronyms are often more commonly used in English, even for monolingual Spanish speakers. For example, the acronym COPD (chronic obstructive pulmonary disease) is often more understood when presented in English than when presented as its Spanish equivalent EPOC; HMO is often more used than its Spanish equivalent, *organización del mantenimiento de la salud*; and technical terms such as *bronchodilators* are often more understood than their Spanish translations.

Translation alone is not sufficient to make the meaning of quality information clear to all users. Some terms are better understood in English than in Spanish.

- The notion of "strangers coming into their home" to provide home health services raised concern for some Spanish-speaking participants, because it goes against the cultural tradition of the family providing care, until they were assured that these services would be provided with the recommendation of their doctor.

Other issues include misinterpreting phrases or terms related to quality of care, such as equating "communicate well" with providers being able to speak Spanish or "quality ratings" ("*calificaciones del plan,*" in Spanish) as denoting eligibility, or "qualifying" for a plan.

In addition, for younger or bilingual consumers, some terms are better understood, or more commonly used, in English than Spanish. For example, adult children or caregivers who are bilingual may prefer to use English language versions of written material or websites when reviewing information for their own use but may choose to view Spanish language versions of those same materials when assisting monolingual parents. In addition, several technical terms or acronyms are often more commonly used in English, even for monolingual Spanish speakers. For example, the acronym COPD (chronic obstructive pulmonary disease) is often more understood when presented in English than when presented as its Spanish equivalent EPOC; HMO is often more used than its Spanish equivalent, *organización del mantenimiento de la salud*; and technical terms such as *bronchodilators* are often more understood than their Spanish translations.

V. Usability and Navigation

Our research has also focused on evaluating the usability of the *Compare* tools, assessing users' ability to navigate, understand, and use the quality information on these tools. Usability, or user experience, focuses on having a deep understanding of users — what they need, what they value, their abilities, and also their limitations. As described above, we know consumers are most interested in information relevant to their particular tasks, needs, and circumstances. They want that information to be presented in formats that make it easy to find and use but that also provide a level of detail that makes the information useful. Although there are differences among the *Compare* tools to accommodate the different types of provider/plan comparisons, any website should be designed to allow users to complete the task or goal they set out to complete. Websites that have the user experience in mind support the completion of the user's task by having intentional and obvious pathways to lead them to their goal. More important, those who oversee policy and regulations for the *Compare* tools may have differing goals or objectives than the user, and this mismatch often leads to poor user experience. For example, the team has found that the *Plan Finder* has been optimized for information intermediaries (in addition to trying to cover stand-alone drug plans, health plans with drug coverage, and health plans without drug coverage), resulting in poor user experience for beneficiaries and their caregivers.

> Those who oversee policy for the Compare tools may have different objectives than website users and this mismatch can lead to poor user experience.

When the research team was asked by CMS to evaluate the *Compare* tools, we used the following key principles in our assessment of best practices in optimizing user experience. Items related to usability and navigation include the following:

Context

- Make the purpose and usefulness of the site immediately obvious
- Give users a framework for understanding what is being measured

Presentation and Display

- Use language that consumers can readily understand
- Make it easy for users to find the information they want
- Include meaningful link labels
- Use well-designed headings to help users scan and read written material

Ease of Use/Decision Support

- Minimize cognitive burden (help consumers process and synthesize information)
- Help users integrate information to make a decision

- Tailor information for different consumer audiences and the tasks they seek to undertake

Although we have not conducted recent usability testing of the *Compare* tools in their present form (the tools have changed over the years with the addition of new content and implementation of a consistent design), we have identified some overall themes through our research related to usability navigation that remain relevant.

Context

CMS periodically makes enhancements or changes to the *Compare* tools. For example, in June 2012, CMS redesigned *Hospital Compare* to add new measures and organize the information using a tab structure. Although the redesign of the *Compare* tools has simplified navigation by requiring fewer steps to access information on quality and performance measures, it eliminated some contextual information that existed in earlier versions that provided users with a *clear sense of the site's purpose and content*. These include navigational cues required by users to understand the tools' full potential. As a result, users remain unaware of the breadth of information available in the tools or that they are designed to enable users to conduct a side-by-side comparison of hospitals, home health agencies, or health plans.

The information that currently appears above the fold on the home page of each tool, including the heading "Find a [insert provider type]" directly above the search box, effectively conveys that the *Compare* tools can be used to search for providers or plans by location. Our research indicated that most users approach the tools as a way to generate a list of available hospitals/agencies/ plans, often stopping upon reaching the initial Results page. For example, when evaluating the usability of the sites, we found that few users were aware that quality data existed in the *Plan Finder* and *Home Health Compare* tools, and most users did not access the quality data or the Compare page on their own. Instead, consumers and professionals thought the data available on the Results page — such as provider name, location, and basic provider characteristics — represented the full extent of available data on the tool. They also thought the "compare" feature was represented in the way the information was displayed on the Results page, because they could view the same type of information for multiple providers at one time. When prompted, users found the functionality to compare up to three providers (for example, hospitals or agencies) very useful in helping to constrain the often large number of available options.

In addition to providing users with information on the purpose and the information available on the *Compare* tools, it is helpful to give users an *overarching framework to understand what to expect and how the information on the sites is organized.* We conducted formative research around the potential use of the IOM's six aims for improvement and the six quality domains of the National Quality Strategy as a potential conceptual or organizational framework for reporting hospital quality and efficiency measures on *Hospital Compare.* Participants understood the underlying concepts and found them to be a useful way to conceptualize *quality* in the health care setting.

During this same research, the team introduced *Hospital Compare* to participants and briefly explored their response to it, in the context of discussions earlier in that research around health care quality. Because the website had just been redesigned to include a tab-based navigation design, rather than quality measures listed as either *process of care* or *outcomes of care* measures, the team was able to probe on whether the recently revised format and tab structure facilitated users' understanding of the information on the site. Earlier research consistently found that several features of the old *Hospital Compare* format made the website difficult for consumers to navigate and understand.

Most users approach the tools as a way to generate a list of providers, stopping after the initial Results page.

Overall, participants understood the new tab structure and organization of the site, identified areas of interest, and seemed less overwhelmed by the volume of information than was the case in prior consumer research. They also understood that three of the tab labels — Patient Survey Results, Timely and Effective Care, and Readmissions, Complications, and Deaths — related to the IOM quality domains previously discussed, which were also the three topic areas of most interest to them. Although, as in prior research, participants were interested in Patient Survey Results, most were at least equally interested in the other two categories. When asked to compare these three tab labels to the corresponding IOM domain labels, most thought that labels on the website better captured the kind of information that was being conveyed.

Consistent with previous findings, however, participants had difficulty interpreting the remaining three tab labels — Use of Medical Imaging,

Medicare Payment, and Number of Medicare Patients. Most participants assumed that the Use of Medical Imaging tab would show information about the availability of specific imaging services; however, when they looked at the measures under this tab more closely, a few participants recognized that they reflected potential overuse of medical imaging, consistent with the IOM concept of avoiding waste. Participants expressed little interest in the Medicare Payment and Number of Medicare Patients tabs, which they did not associate with questions about quality.

These findings, although specific to *Hospital Compare*, indicate that CMS has made great strides in improving the design of its *Compare* tools and thus providing users with a better framework for understanding what information is included.

Presentation and Display

Overall, the *Compare* tools do a good job of providing information in plain language. Some of the tools, such as *Hospital Compare* and *Plan Finder*, organize the information in clearly labeled categories (rather than lengthy lists of individual measures) to help users navigate the site. However, some of the tools include pages that are content heavy and/or require a lot of scrolling; link labels could be used more effectively to aide navigation through the tools. For example, although the quality measures on *Home Health Compare* are grouped into five overarching categories, such as "Managing Daily Activities" and "Preventing Harm," the default display is to expand each category and have all of the measures visible. This requires the user to scroll down the page to determine available information and identify pertinent content, rather than detect relevant information at a glance.

Additionally, the *Compare* sites sometimes provide key information below the fold. Many users are unaware they need to scroll down the page, and they often do not access this important information. This issue is most problematic when viewing the Results page and Compare page for each tool. Elderly website users may typically use a lower screen resolution for larger screen images, which would further limit the information seen above the fold.

Ease of Use/Decision Support

The *Compare* tools are effective resources in determining which hospitals, home health agencies, dialysis facilities, nursing homes, or health plans are available in or serve a given area, as well as in identifying certain features and quality data for a particular provider or plan. All of the tools use some visual displays (graphic displays, star ratings, pop-up explanations), guidance on directionality, and benchmarks to help users make sense of individual measures and discrete data. For example, *Plan Finder* uses icons on the Results page that denote high and low performance plans, enabling users to identify these plans at a glance. The tools also provide links to explanatory text that is useful to understanding and correctly interpreting the quality measures (for example, "What is this?" or "Why is this important?" explanations) from multiple points, improving user access to this information. However, the *Compare* tools' current design limits their utility as decision support tools for consumers. Several areas in which the tools could be improved to support provider/plan choice decisions are described below.

Tools tend to lack effective methods for narrowing results. For some tools, such as *Home Health Compare* and *Hospital Compare*, the initial results pages do not include the types of information, such as summary ratings, that would facilitate narrowing options in a meaningful way; instead, users are only able to limit results by physical address, provider name, and services offered/hospital type. In many instances, users are unable to limit their results to a manageable number, despite using the available filters. For example, an initial search for home health agencies in Chicago, Illinois, yields 669 agencies. Using the "Services Provided" filter to keep only agencies that offer all services eliminates 59 agencies, leaving 610 results. A user would then need to randomly select three providers at a time from among the 610 to access information, such as quality data, that could them help select a provider. The inability to narrow based on information such as quality impedes the effective use of quality information in the decision-making process.

The inability to narrow a search impedes the effective use of quality information for decision-making.

Plan Finder does include the types of "meaningful" information on the results page that is lacking from some of the other tools; however, the filters themselves hinder users' ability to effectively narrow their results. The most significant issue is that the filters appear on the page prior to the initial results page, and users often either overlook the filters or do not feel ready to use them before they have seen their results. When users proceed to the initial results page, there are no filters available to them, and we have rarely seen a research participant return to the previous step to use the filters. Additionally, when asked to use the filter feature, most participants did not click on the "Update Results" button, which is required for some of the filters to take effect. For example, *Plan Finder* users did not realize that results were not immediately updated upon selecting a value, and they did not realize they had to click on the "Update Results" button for the filter to work. Instead, they would adjust the filter and then click on the "Continue to Plan Results" button. Clicking on this button sometimes updated the plan results and sometimes did not. Several *Home Health Compare* users clicked on the "New Search" button instead of "Update Results," which brought them back to the *Home Health Compare* home page. They explained that they were unfamiliar with the "Update Results" terminology and did not know what would happen if they clicked on that button.

Information is not filtered or focused by the specific tasks tool users want to accomplish. During our research, most users would initially state they were interested in viewing the quality ratings for the plans/agencies/hospitals. Upon closer examination, though, the typical user became overwhelmed by the volume of information and was not sure what to make of it or how to use it. This was particularly apparent during testing of *Home Health Compare*, which does not offer a summary or composite rating for agencies. Users struggled to develop an overall assessment from the individual quality measures as well as determine how two or more agencies compared when one agency scored better on some measures and worse on others.

The *Plan Finder* results include a summary rating of quality, but also include many different types of cost and benefits information, which poses several challenges to consumers, including the following:

- Because of space constraints, the labels for the information are generally not detailed enough for consumer audiences to fully understand the meaning of the information.
- Each cell in the results page includes several types of information, making it difficult for users to skim the page to compare specific elements.
- There are too many different types of information for a consumer to integrate to effectively narrow their results.

Tool design is not always optimized for consumer audiences. All of the Compare tools have multiple audiences, including consumers, intermediaries, and providers, and it is simply not possible to optimize them for every possible type of user. If CMS considers the primary audience for the tools to be consumers, or if the agency would like to increase and improve consumer use, then the tools should be optimized for the consumer user.

The results page of the Plan Finder, which we described above, provides a good illustration of this issue. Because intermediaries, such as State Health Insurance Assistance Program counselors and 1-800-MEDICARE customer service representatives, find it helpful to minimize "clicks" and see more information on a single page, the format and comprehensiveness of the initial results page is well-suited to them. Not surprisingly, our research with intermediaries indicates that they tend to be satisfied with the tool. But the cost of adding more information to support intermediary use contributes to a results page that is difficult for consumers to use. A more consumer-friendly tool would limit information on the initial results — providing the elements CMS deems most important for narrowing plans to a manageable number — and then would make the more detailed information available in later pages, such as the side-by-side comparison or plan profile. Such an approach would help consumers narrow plans and prioritize information, while still making the detailed information available.

Tools could provide more-customized results. Because users access the *Compare* tools for a variety of tasks and reasons, CMS may want to explore expanding the tools' decision-support capabilities to enable tailored sessions based on who the user is and/or the purpose of his/her search. Allowing users to input what they are looking for at the beginning of a session will likely increase the perceived utility of the tools. Potential data sources that could provide insight on the range of user goals could include data collected from the 1-800-MEDICARE call center, State Health Insurance Assistance Programs, ForeSee Surveys or Google Analytics.

Enabling tailored sessions based on users' specific needs can expand the Compare tools' decision-support capabilities.

End Notes

[1] See, for example, https://cahps.ahrq.gov/consumer-reporting/talkingquality/, sponsored by the Agency for Healthcare Research and Quality.

[2] Formative and developmental research for CMS's Dialysis Facility Compare was conducted by RTI International.

[3] This is supported by several recent systematic research reviews. See, in particular, Totten, A. M., J. Wagner, A. Tiwari, et al., Closing the Quality Gap: Revisiting the State of the Science (Vol. 5: Public Reporting as a Quality Improvement Strategy), Rockville MD: Agency for Healthcare Research and Quality, July 2012 (Evidence Reports/Technology Assessments, No. 208.5.); and Fung, C. H., Y. W. Lim, S. Mattke, C. Damberg, and P. G. Shekelle, "Systematic Review: The Evidence That Publishing Patient Care Performance Data Improves Quality of Care," Annals of Internal Medicine, 2008, 148(2):111–123.

[4] See, for example, Lamb, G. C., M. A. Smith, W. B. Weeks, and C. Queram, "Publicly Reported Quality-Of-Care Measures Influenced Wisconsin Physician Groups to Improve Performance," Health Affairs, 2013, 32(3):536–543; and Hibbard, J. H., J. Stockard, and M. Tusler, "Does Publicizing Hospital Performance Stimulate Quality Improvement Efforts?" Health Affairs, 2003, 22(2):84–94.

[5] For a summary of criteria used by the oversight organizations such as the Agency for Healthcare Research and Quality (AHRQ), the National Quality Forum, and The Joint Commissions, see "Appendix A: Measure Evaluation Framework: Selecting Quality and Resource Use Measures: A Decision Guide for Community Quality Collaboratives," Rockville, MD: AHRQ, May 2010, available at [http://www.ahrq.gov/professionals/quality-patient-safety/quality-resources/tools/perfmeasguide/perfmeasappa.html].

[6] Institute of Medicine. Crossing the Quality Chasm: A New Health System for the 21st Century, Washington, DC: National Academy Press, 2001.

[7] U.S. Department of Health & Human Services. "Report to Congress. National Strategy for Quality Improvement in Health Care," Washington, DC, March 2011.

[8] See, for example, Hibbard, J. H., J. Greene, and D. Daniel, "What Is Quality Anyway? Performance Reports that Clearly Communicate to Consumers the Meaning of Quality of Care," Medical Care Research and Review, vol. 67, 2010, pp. 275–293; and Ginsburg, Marjorie, and Kathy Glasmire, "Consumers' Priorities for Hospital Quality Improvement and Implications for Public Reporting," California HealthCare Foundation, April 2011.

INDEX

D

E

F

G

H

I

K

L

M

N

O

S

T

U

V

W

Y